*S*acajawea, a sixteen-year-old Shoshoni Indian girl, and her husband, Toussaint Charbonneau, were hired on as guides and interpreters when the Corps of Discovery led by Meriwether Lewis and William Clark left their winter quarters in the center of North Dakota and began their epic trek to the Pacific Ocean.

Jean Baptiste Charbonneau was about eight weeks old when his mother strapped his cradleboard on her back and the journey began. Young mother and infant endured many hardships on the history-making trip.

The physically abused young mother proved to be "indepensable" to the success of one of the greatest explorations in all of American history. Her negotiation skills, translation abilities, awareness of Indian culture, familiarity with the territory and its flora and fauna, and her almost daily provision of roots, berries, and herbs made her a respected member of the group.

Since the end of the expedition, much has been written about this amazing teenager. Unfortunately most of the writings are full of myth, legend, and historically inaccurate information.

Confusion about Sacajawea's valuable role evaporates when the source of the facts about her—The Lewis and Clark Journals—are consulted. The two captains wrote much about her contributions as they carefully and precisely documented all events of the expedition.

The Truth about Sacajawea is an accurate paraphrase of the journal accounts that mention Sacajawea or "the Sqar," as she was often called. This entry-by-entry approach allows readers to experience what the explorers wrote about Sacajawea. Between the journal accounts is a short commentary and brief synopsis of events that took place between the entries.

The concise, clear, and accurate account of the twenty-one months Sacajawea spent with Lewis and Clark is a reliable picture of this quietly resourceful teenager and the enormous contributions she made to this famous expedition.

Also by Kenneth Thomasma

Naya Nuki: Shoshoni Girl Who Ran
Soun Tetoken: Nez Perce Boy Tames a Stallion
Om-kas-toe: Blackfeet Twin Captures an Elkdog
Kunu: Winnebago Boy Escapes
Pathki Nana: Kootenai Girl Solves a Mystery
Moho Wat: Sheepeater Boy Attempts a Rescue
Amee-nah: Zuni Boy Runs the Race of His Life
Doe Sia: Bannock Girl Saves a Handcart Pioneer

The Truth about

Sacajawea

Ken Thomasma
5/26/2000

Kenneth Thomasma
Agnes Vincen Talbot, Illustrator

Grandview Publishing Company
Jackson, Wyoming 83001

©1997 by Kenneth Thomasma

Published by Grandview Publishing Company
Box 2863, Jackson, WY 83001
Fax: 1-307-734-0210
Phone: 1-800-525-7344
e-mail: kenthomasma@blissnet.com

Printed in the United States of America

ISBN: 1880114-16-X Hardcover
ISBN: 1880114-18-6 Paperback

Dr. Gary E. Moulton, Editor of *The Journals of the Lewis & Clark Expedition* (Lincoln, Neb.: University of Nebraska Press, 1987) has graciously allowed me to use his material as the basis for the paraphrase entries containing references to Sacajawea. Dr. Moulton has also given permission to use three of his maps that document the expedition's route to the Pacific Ocean.

A special thank you to Dr. Jack DeForest, Environmental Economist, who reviewed the first edition of THE TRUTH ABOUT SACAJAWEA and suggested the addition of the Quick Reference Guide which has made the book even more useful to serious readers and students of this teenage mother's part in the epic exploration initiated by President Thomas Jefferson.

First printing, June 1997 (Hardcover)   First printing, April 1998 (Paperback)
Second printing, January 2000 (Hardcover)   Second printing, May 1999 (Paperback)

To
**Sacajawea's descendants
the Lemhi Shoshoni people**

At a critical point
August 13—31, 1805
in Lemhi Valley, Idaho
the Lemhi Shoshoni sold horses to the explorers
and provided them with a guide
to make it possible for the expedition
to cross the Rocky Mountains
and continue on to the Pacific Ocean.

Lewis and Clark made many promises in return for the help of the Indian people. The Lemhi Shoshoni were promised peace and prosperity from the great white chief. Along with the Nez Perce people on the Columbia River drainage, the Lemhi Shoshoni provided essential assistance to the expedition.

One hundred years after Lewis and Clark left the Lemhi Valley, the Lemhi Shoshoni people were forced from their ancestral lands and moved two hundred miles south to the Fort Hall Reservation.

Now the Lemhi Shoshoni people dream of a return to their sacred homeland. There they want to establish the Sacajawea Cultural Interpretive Center. When visitors come in 2003-2006 to celebrate the bicentennial of the epic journey of the Lewis and Clark Expedition, the Lemhi Shoshoni want to be there to welcome them.

The proper recognition of Sacajawea, her descendants, and all Indian women will become a reality. Grandview Publishing is donating the profits from this book to help these dreams come true.

Contents

A Message from The Lemhi Shoshoni People

We, the Lemhi Shoshoni, have our unique ideas regarding Sacajawea of Lewis and Clark fame. We view Sacajawea as a representative member of our culture. We are proud she used special skills to help Lewis and Clark survive in the early 1800s.

Sacajawea's mother nurtured her from birth. As the young girl grew, her mother expertly and carefully taught her daughter to find and preserve food, make clothing, construct shelters, care for children, and pack for travel to distant hunting grounds. As Lewis and Clark learned, Sacajawea had a great many skills. They also learned she was able to stay calm and act wisely during life-threatening times. Her expert care for her firstborn child made an impression on them.

Like all of us, Sacajawea was molded by her family, her tribal members, and her experiences. To us she represents all that is good about our people, the Lemhi Shoshoni. Some native people criticize Sacajawea for helping the majority culture travel through our lands and eventually dominate us completely. However, we realize Sacajawea was only eleven years old when she was captured by enemy warriors and taken away to be sold into slavery. She was a teenager when Lewis and Clark enlisted her and her husband to help them travel to and from the Pacific Ocean.

The explorers came to Sacajawea first and eventually to our people with glowing promises of peace and prosperity. How could sixteen-year-old Sacajawea or our people foresee what the future actually held for them and all native people? We know Sacajawea did what she thought was correct. We know from all the words written about her that she was an outstanding human being. Surely we cannot blame this young Shoshoni mother for the inability to see into the future.

In 1812 the clerk at Fort Manuel wrote in the log book, "This evening the wife of Charbonneau, a Snake* squaw, died of putrid fever. She was a good and best woman in the fort."

Thus we honor Sacajawea for who she was—not for what she did to help Lewis and Clark. We know she was a good woman and a fine mother. For these things we proudly want the world to know Sacajawea is Lemhi Shoshoni.

We are happy that for the first time people can read a book that tells exactly what Sacajawea did during her twenty-one months with Lewis and Clark.

Representing the Fort Lemhi Indian Community
Rod Ariwite
January 1997

*The term *Snake* is used when referring to Shoshoni Indian people. It is believed it came into use as a result of sign language. When signing basket weaving by a hand movement, the sign was misread as a snake slithering along.

Preface

When Sacajawea's descendants, the Lemhi Shoshoni of Fort Hall, Idaho, searched for written material about their famous ancestor, they could find nothing suitable to submit to a major Idaho newspaper for background information.

Although so much has been written about Sacajawea (there is even a book which analyzes all the books written about her), a natural history association in Wyoming refuses to sell any books about Sacajawea because they do not pass the test for accuracy and authenticity. Even encyclopedias print incorrect information about her. The cliché, "Don't believe everything you read," certainly applies to Sacajawea. The casual reader will be confused by all this misinformation and will draw false conclusions regarding this teenage Indian mother who traveled with the famous Lewis and Clark Expedition.

In the early 1990s, when I became closely associated with the Lemhi Shoshoni people, I felt the need for a book which will give them and other readers a clear picture of exactly what Sacajawea did during her twenty-one months with Lewis and Clark.

The entry-by-entry approach allows readers to experience what the explorers wrote about Sacajawea. They were the only people who recorded the facts. I accurately paraphrased the entries made by the two captains and their sergeants. Following the entries is a short comment. You may or may not agree with my comments which are recorded only to stimulate thought. Draw your own conclusions. My main purpose is to allow the reader to have the facts in a direct concise format.

Often days or even months elapse between journal entries concerning Sacajawea. To fill in the gaps, I have provided a brief synopsis of events and progress of the expedition as it proceeds toward its goal. These three segments—entry, comment, and synopsis—combine to form a complete, clear picture of Sacajawea and her contribution to American history.

What happened to her after the expedition will always be a topic of much controversy. So will the exact spelling, pronunciation, and meaning of her name. In the Hidatsa Indian language her name is Sakakawea, or Bird Woman. This name is preferred by citizens of North Dakota. The Sacajawea spelling is preferred by Sacajawea's descendants, the Lemhi Shosoni. Irving W. Anderson, nationally recognized expert on the Charbonneau family, has researched the name controversy and feels the most correct spelling is Sacagawea. Out of respect for Sacajawea's descendants, I have elected to use the "j" spelling.

But these issues seem insignificant when compared to this young Lemhi Shoshoni's quiet resourcefulness, her dedication to her firstborn child, and her invaluable contributions to the success of the Lewis and Clark Expedition.

William Clark   Meriwether Lewis

Setting the Stage

*F*or over twenty years a great American had an obsession. Thomas Jefferson longed to know what natural wonders lay west between the Mississippi River and the Pacific Ocean. As a member of the American Philosophical Society, Jefferson and his fellow members wanted to send an expedition to the Pacific Ocean and return. Jefferson was involved in at least three attempts between 1783 and 1800, but none of these efforts materialized.

In 1801 Thomas Jefferson became the third president of a very young United States of America. The new president employed twenty-seven-year-old Meriwether Lewis as his private secretary. In 1802 the president asked young Meriwether to head an expedition from the St. Louis area westward. Jefferson wanted Lewis to explore the Missouri River to its source, find a passage over the mountains, and float the Columbia River drainage to the Pacific Ocean.

Preparations for the grand adventure began almost immediately. First Jefferson and Lewis agreed that a second in command should be chosen in the event something should incapacitate either leader. William Clark, four years older than Lewis, was selected for his military and frontier experience.

The expedition would be organized as an official United States Army unit. The two leaders would be army captains to their men, even though a military red-tape blunder prevented William Clark from receiving that official rank. The project would be called "The Lewis and Clark Expedition."

Captain Lewis immediately prepared for his monumental assignment. He boned up on astronomy, medicine, ethnology, edible plants, and natural history. He made comprehensive lists of supplies, clothing, equipment, medicines, and Indian trade goods. Congress appropriated $2500 for supplies and Indian trade goods. Lewis arranged for construction of a large keelboat to help carry the 3500 pounds of cargo and the crew. The recruitment and training of men would be ongoing from August 1803 through the next winter.

At first the plan was to explain the expedition as merely a literary venture to seek knowledge and enlightenment. This approach would be taken to pacify the Spanish and French authorities who might question the American government's motives for such an endeavor. But in the spring of 1803 Thomas Jefferson closed a deal with the French and made the great land buy now called the Louisanna Purchase. The expedition took on another dramatic purpose. The new goal would emphasize geographic discovery leading to eventual claims on all lands west of the Mississippi River.

The historic expedition was launched up the mighty Missouri River on May 14, 1804. Constant struggles against the powerful current of the Missouri River, hazardous sandbars, snags, and unpredictable weather marked the first season of travel. There were also discipline problems with a few men, a dangerous encounter with Teton Sioux warriors, and the tragic death of Sergeant Charles Floyd from a ruptured appendix.

Covering approximately 1,510 miles in 164 days of travel, on October 25, 1804, the expedition arrived at the Mandan-Hidatsa villages near present-day Bismarck, North Dakota. There on the banks of the Missouri River were five small Indian settlements: two Mandan and three Hidatsa. Men who were involved in fur trading also lived there. Traders and trappers not employed by the companies were called free traders. On November 3, 1804, construction began on Fort Mandan which would serve as winter quarters for the expedition for the next five months.

The very next day, November 4, 1804, a pregnant teenager, Lemhi Shoshoni Sacajawea, walked on to the world stage with her husband, Toussaint Charbonneau. Now the cast of characters is poised for the most dangerous phase of the expedition, the crossing of an unknown and uncharted wilderness.

The Corps of Discovery flotilla will be launched as soon as the ice on the Missouri River breaks up in the spring.

Follow the journal entries about Sacajawea, the Lemhi Shoshoni woman. Discover exactly what she contributed to the overall effort.

The Journal Entries

Sunday, November 4, 1804 <u>*Captain Clark*</u>
A French-Canadian, Toussaint Charbonneau, visits the two explorers. He wants to hire on as an interpreter and guide. Although he has two Shoshoni Indian wives, the explorers engage Charbonneau and one of his wives who would be needed to interpret the Shoshoni language when the explorers entered that territory.

This short entry marks a dramatic turn of events for the expedition. The hiring of Charbonneau and his young Shoshoni wife would prove to be a stroke of good fortune and good judgment.

❖ During the winter the captains meet with traders, Indian leaders, and fur company personnel. They glean as much information as they can about the upper Missouri River, the mountains, and any hint of a water passage to the Pacific Ocean.

Settled in their fort, the men set to work constructing canoes from large trees in the area. Although the average night time temperature is zero or below, Indian men regularly spend the night in the open covered with a buffalo skin. Seemingly they suffer no ill results.

On December 7, Captain Lewis leads a buffalo hunt resulting in the killing of eleven buffalo. The next day nine buffalo are killed. The men eat only the tongues and leave the rest for scavengers. They say they are living off the fat of the land.

Monday, February 11, 1805 <u>*Captain Lewis*</u>

About 5 P.M. Sacajawea, one of the wives of Charbonneau, gives birth to her firstborn, a fine boy. It was a tedious labor, marked with violent pain. Rene Jessaume, a free trader Lewis found living with the Mandans, tells Lewis that a small amount of the rattle from a rattlesnake will hasten the birth. Captain Lewis has such a rattle. He gives it to Jessaume who breaks off two rings of the rattle, grinds them up, mixes them in water, and gives the drink to Sacajawea. Ten minutes later she gives birth to Jean Baptiste Charbonneau. Lewis isn't sure the rattle truly helped with the birth, but feels the remedy might be worth further study.

Sixteen-year-old Sacajawea gave birth to Jean Baptiste at Fort Mandan on a clear cold day. The infant would be carried by Sacajawea all the way to the Pacific Ocean. She would prove to be a diligent mother and caregiver under trying and hazardous conditions.

❖ The captains keep written records of the daily weather conditions. The temperature on many days is below zero with dangerous windchills of sixty to eighty degrees below zero. The Indian people bring their horses into their lodges during the most severe weather. As winter settles in on the fort there is very little hunting success. Trading goods and services for corn helps the expedition survive during the winter.

Captains Lewis and Clark engage Toussaint Charbonneau as an interpreter and guide. Sacajawea, Charbonneau's wife, watches as the men negotiate. Mandan Indian homes are in the background.

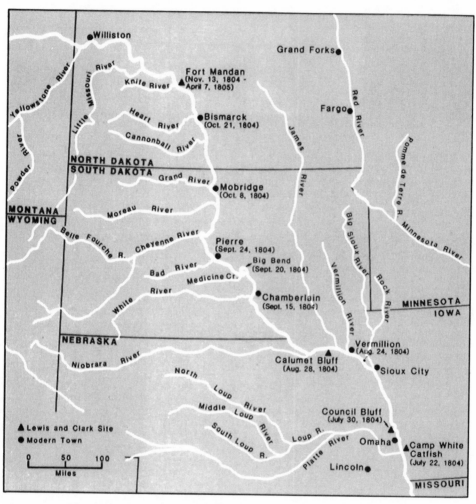

The Expedition's Route, August 25, 1804–April 6, 1805

Private Shields is a skilled blacksmith and uses scrap metal to fashion tools for the Indian people. He trades tools for corn. Captains Lewis and Clark provide medical treatment and the Indians pay them with corn.

Captain Lewis treats a thirteen-year-old boy for frost-bitten feet. After trying for sixteen days to save the toes, Lewis has to amputate them to save the boy's life. No surgical tools are available, so Lewis probably uses a handsaw.

Monday, March 11, 1805 <u>*Captain Clark*</u>
A problem arises between the explorers and Charbonneau. Charbonneau may back out and leave the expedition, taking Sacajawea with him. He is being given the night to decide whether or not he is going on with the explorers. They suspect interference from the fur-trading companies who want to protect their control of the fur trade by sabotaging the expedition.

Evidently the discipline of an army unit did not appeal to Charbonneau and he balks at the duty requirements of the expedition. The Hudson Bay and Northwest Fur Companies had some of their men in the Fort Mandan area. The captains suspect the fur companies are influencing Charbonneau, although they cannot prove it. Most evidence points to Charbonneau's personal preferences as the problem area. It is believed he thinks the captains will give in to his demands because of Sacajawea's potential value as an interpreter and negotiator with the Indians when horses will be needed.

It is decided to have two large pirogues (large canoelike boats) constructed to carry most of the heavy cargo. The cumbersome keelboat can be sent back to St. Louis.

Tuesday, March 12, 1805 <u>Captain Clark</u>
Charbonneau decides to quit the expedition. He does not like the prospect of having to stand guard duty. He does not want to be told which personal items he will be allowed to take. If he didn't like any man, he wanted to be free to quit. Charbonneau's demands are unreasonable, and because the agreement made was verbal, he is free to leave.

The keelboat

Thursday, March 14, 1805 Sergeant Ordway
Charbonneau and his family move out of Fort
Mandan. He erects his buffalo-hide lodge nearby.

> **Should this abrupt separation become permanent, the course of history will be changed dramatically.**

❖ The weather turns mild and the river begins rising. The men are busy shucking corn and bagging it for the trip. Work on the canoes is stepped up as the ice on the river begins to break up.

Sunday, March 17, 1805 Captain Clark
One of the French-speaking men has a message
from Charbonneau who now promises to do every-
thing the explorers demand of him if he may rejoin the
expedition. He is sorry for his foolishness. In a
face-to-face meeting with the captains Charbonneau
agrees to all the terms of employment and is taken back
into the service of the United States of America.

> **It is believed that Francois Labiche delivered Charbonneau's message. The meeting between the explorers and Charbonneau must have been a dramatic, emotional one and takes place just three weeks prior to the launch of the flotilla for the journey up the Missouri River. The restoration of Charbonneau indicates how much the two captains want Charbonneau and Sacajewea's services.**

❖ As the weather continues to warm up, the captains closely monitor the breakup of the ice on the mighty Missouri River. Final preparations for departure are almost completed. All the information about the upper Missouri River country that can be obtained is gathered from every possible source, including Indians and trappers who are in the Fort Mandan area. The captains spend hours and hours with the Mandans and Hidatsas talking about peace.

Tuesday, April 1, 1805 Captain Clark
Preparations begin to break camp and head up the Missouri River. Charbonneau will take his two wives with him. Charbonneau speaks to his wives in Hidatsa. That means Sacajawea will speak to Shoshoni people in their language, translate it into Hidatsa for Charbonneau who will translate it into French for Labiche, and Labiche will translate it into English for the captains.

This is mysterious. Was Charbonneau planning to take both wives? Did language difficulties cause a breakdown in communications. Did something happen between April 1 and 7 that resulted in only Sacajawea accompanying the expedition? Nothing was written to solve this mystery. What might have happened if both of Charbonneau's wives made the journey?

❖ The coming of spring is welcomed by all the explorers. Never had they lived through such a cold and hazardous winter. Now they are excited and eager to be on their way to the unknown. Every night Cruzatte takes out his fiddle and the men dance for hours.

During the final week in Fort Mandan, the weather is cold and rainy. Last-minute preparations are completed for the keelboat's trip back to St. Louis. The two pirogues are ready for loading. Six other canoes are ready to launch. The river is free of ice.

Thirty-one men, one woman, and one infant make up the party to the Pacific Ocean. Included are the two captains, three sergeants, twenty-three privates, interpreter Drewyer who is an expert in Indian sign language, Captain Clark's slave York, and the Charbonneau family.

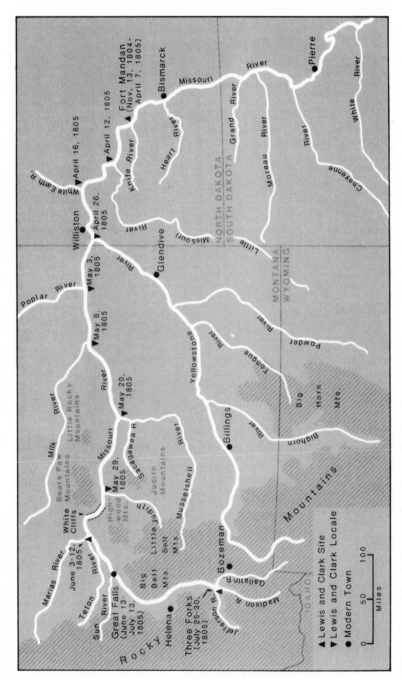

The Expedition's Route, April 7–July 27, 1805

Fort Mandan (Nov. 13, 1804–April 7, 1805)

April 12, 1805
April 16, 1805
April 26, 1805
May 3, 1805
May 8, 1805
May 20, 1805
May 29, 1805
June 3-12, 1805
June 13–July 13, 1805
Three Forks (July 26-30, 1805)

Bismarck
Pierre
Williston
Glendive
Billings
Bozeman
Great Falls
Helena

Missouri River
White River
Grand River
Moreau River
Cheyenne River
Little Missouri River
Knife River
Heart River
White Earth R.
Poplar River
Milk River
Yellowstone River
Powder River
Tongue River
Big Horn Mts.
Bighorn River
Musselshell River
Judith Mountains
Sacagawea R.
Missouri River
Little Rocky Mountains
Bears Paw Mountains
White Cliffs
Highwood Mts.
Little Belt Mts.
Big Belt Mts.
Marias River
Teton River
Sun River
Gallatin R.
Madison R.
Jefferson R.
Rocky Mountains

NORTH DAKOTA
SOUTH DAKOTA
MONTANA
WYOMING
IDAHO

▲ Lewis and Clark Site
▼ Lewis and Clark Locale
● Modern Town

0   50   100
Miles

Lewis writes President Jefferson a long letter describing the situation and plans for the remainder of the expedition. The captain hopes he can reach the Pacific Ocean and return to the headwaters of the Missouri before winter comes, maybe even make it all the way back to Fort Mandan. In reality the expedition would just barely make it to the Pacific Ocean before winter closed in on the mountains.

Sunday, April 7, 1805 Captains Lewis and Clark

At 4 P.M. the expedition gets underway. The names of the people in the expedition are listed, including Charbonneau and his wife Sacajawea who carries her two-month-old son in a cradleboard.

After a short day, the red and white pirogues and six canoes are pulled over for the first camp.

Captain Lewis

The two captains, Charbonneau, Sacajawea, and Jean Baptiste sleep in a shelter made of tanned buffalo hides sewn together with sinew to fit around the cone-shaped lodge.

The detailed description of the shelter indicates it to be a plains Indian style tipi. The pattern of the Charbonneau family and the two captains being together during much of the trip fell into place the very first day. It is believed that Sacajawea was to remain close to the captains to prevent any unwanted incident between the men and the only woman in the expedition. The tipi wore out before the expedition returned. Charbonneau would receive compensation for its use. With a sense of pride Captain Lewis describes his little flotilla. He contemplates

the great mission he and his small contingent are embarking on and expresses his anxiety for the safety and success of each member as they venture into an uncharted wilderness. Lewis said this had to be the happiest day of his life. He even mentioned that his flotilla of six small canoes and two larger pirogues, though not quite as respectable as the vessels of Columbus and Captain Cook, nevertheless were viewed by him with as much pleasure as those famous men viewed their sailing ships.

❖ The first mishap occurs on April 8. High winds whip up the water and one small canoe fills with water. The only thirty pounds of gunpowder not sealed against water and half a bag of biscuits get wet. This would not be the only encounter with trouble on the river.

Detailed descriptions of plants and creatures begin to appear in the entries.

Tuesday, April 9, 1805 Captain Lewis
When they pull over for supper, Sacajawea immediately searches for food. She takes a sharp stick and begins digging in the ground near small piles of driftwood. She knows mice hide large quantities of roots in these locations. Soon Sacajawea gathers a good supply of what Lewis calls edible wild artichoke roots and a detailed description of the root appears in the journal.

It did not take long for Sacajawea to demonstrate her skill at gathering edible plants. There is some doubt that these roots were artichoke.
Sacajawea's training in food gathering had started at the very young age of three when she would have been helping her

25

mother pick berries, dig roots, collect seeds, and dry meat. By her teen years she would be an accomplished food gatherer. Teenage Sacajawea would already possess all the skills of a working woman and be expected to bear and raise children at the same time.

Indian women were the fabric of their culture. They worked from dawn to dark gathering food, preparing it for storage, scraping and curing hides, erecting shelters, making bedding and clothing, caring for children, and accompanying hunters to help butcher the kills made.

While her young son sleeps, Sacajawea gathers roots near the base of the woodpile. Almost daily she enriched the menu with berries, herbs, and roots.

❖ Almost immediately the explorers report attacks by mosquitoes. These pests would be a major source of torment during most of the journey.

Captain Lewis is alarmed by large sections of riverbank breaking away and posing a hazard to the small flotilla. Detailed records of geography, flora and fauna, and the weather appear in his journal.

Captain Clark assumes the mapmaking duties.

Saturday, April 13, 1805 <u>Captain Lewis</u>
Under a favorable wind at 9 A.M., two sails are hoisted on the white pirogue. At 2 P.M. without warning a sudden blast of wind hits the craft and rolls it onto its side. Charbonneau, who is at the helm, in sheer panic turns the pirogue broadside to the wind. The boat nearly capsizes. Fortunately the wind lets up for a few seconds. Lewis shouts for Drewyer to take the helm from Charbonneau. The sails are quickly lowered—a lucky escape from disaster.

This accident would have cost them dearly. The white pirogue, the expedition's flagship, was considered their safest vessel. It carried their valuable instruments, papers, medicines, and the finest merchandise for trade with Indian people. Also on board were both captains, three men who could not swim, and Sacajawea with her baby. Being two hundred yards from shore, a capsizing in the high waves certainly would have meant loss of life.

It is interesting to note that the Charbonneau family is on the safest boat along with the captains and the most valuable cargo items. This would not be the only incident that indicates Charbonneau's great fear of water.

❖ The expedition made almost one hundred miles of progress the first four days. By April 15 the expedition finally entered unexplored territory.

The men report the first sighting of the whitebear or grizzly. They also tell of seeing an abundance of big game animals: buffalo, deer, elk, and antelope. Hunting is excellent and fresh meat is plentiful.

The discovery of discarded whisky kegs indicates the British practice of using alcohol to induce the Assiniboin people (a large tribe living on the plains of Montana and Canada, and related to the Sioux) to trade with them.

Thursday, April 18, 1805 Captain Clark
After noticing early in the day that the river made a great bend south, Clark and the Charbonneau family cut across by land, a two-mile walk, and easily arrive at the river before the boats. Because Charbonneau is not feeling well, Clark leaves the family to do some hunting. He is able to bag one deer and one elk.

The meandering river allowed this overland shortcut. Some days the expedition would stop to camp, climb the riverbank, and see the previous night's camp just a short distance back. They would travel ten to fifteen miles by river and gain less than five miles by land. The twisting river added many miles to the journey.

❖ The explorers come upon the first burial platform. Prairie Indians bury their dead in dead trees or on a platform because they believe the Great Spirit will come and take the deceased to the Spiritland.

The captains observe tons of soil blowing through the air like giant clouds. The power of the wind was impressive. High winds would prove to be life-threatening on more than one occasion.

On April 25 the group made camp on the banks of the Yellowstone River. The area had abundant herds of buffalo, elk, deer, and antelope. The explorers enjoy eating buffalo tongue and bone marrow.

Joseph Fields was sent to explore the Yellowstone River as far as he could go easily. Indian people had reported the Yellowstone River was passable by canoe all the way to the mountains. No record is made of Sacajawea being asked about the Yellowstone River. Had the expedition followed the Yellowstone River, as much as two months' time would have been saved. It is believed Lewis stayed with the Missouri River route because President Jefferson had given orders to follow the Missouri to its source.

Four days later, on April 29, Lewis shoots a grizzly bear which takes off after him. Because the bear is slowed by his wound, Lewis is able to run one hundred yards, reload the gun, and fire off a fatal shot. The ferocity of the great grizzly bear would astound the men again and again.

Tuesday, April 30, 1805 Captain Clark
At sunrise, when Clark and the Charbonneau family start out on land, Sacajawea finds a currant-like bush which she says produces a delicious fruit. She says there were many bushes like this in the mountains.

Taking the time to record this incident is another indication that the explorers were impressed with Sacajawea's knowledge of edible plants. Back in the Lemhi Valley her skills would have been commonplace and not worthy of special attention. No doubt the Indian woman enjoyed the appreciation shown by the explorers.

❖ On May 2, snow falls until ten o'clock, reaching an inch in depth. Ice covers the water pails. Buffalo are everywhere. Clark and Drewyer kill a grizzly bear. Although it is hit with ten shots, the great bear is able to swim to a sandbar halfway across the river. It sits there for twenty minutes before it dies. Five balls are found in its lungs and five others are scattered throughout its body.

Wednesday, May 8, 1805 <u>Captain Clark</u>
As Clark and the Charbonneau family walk
along the shore, Sacajawea stops and begins gather-
ing roots from the hillside. One root is wild licorice.
The captain tastes a second specimen — a white apple
root, a kind of breadroot.

Here is another mention of Sacajawea's ability to find food. The addition of roots and berries to the daily diet would be beneficial to the health of expedition members and also that of young Jean Baptiste.

❖ The captains report losing a whole afternoon of travel because of dangerously high winds. The violent winds continue the next morning so the expedition cannot not proceed until 1 P.M.

On May 14 six men stalk a giant grizzly bear. They critically wound the animal. The enraged bear charges the hunters, sending four men into the river in the attempt to escape. The maddened bear plunges in after them. Two men who had taken refuge in a canoe quickly reload, fire, and finally kill the great beast.

Tuesday, May 14, 1805 <u>Captain Lewis</u>
There was an even more frightening incident the
same day. Toward evening Charbonneau, probably
one of the most timid watermen in the world, is at the
helm of the white pirogue while the two captains take a
customary walk along the shore. A tremendous burst
of wind strikes the pirogue broadside while it is under
sail. Once again instead of turning the boat into the
wind, Charbonneau holds it broadside to the wind.
The powerful wind yanks the sail from the hand of the
man holding it. The large pirogue rolls on its side.

It would have gone all the way over had the oarsmen not dug in their oars to stabilize the vessel.

Both captains fire their rifles to get the panic-stricken crew's attention and order them to cut the sail loose. The shots are not heard in the roaring gale. The boat heaves over precariously for thirty seconds.

Just in time the crew lowers the sail and is able to right the pirogue which is filled with water to within an inch of the gunwales and is on the verge of sinking. Through it all Charbonneau just sits there in shock and cries to his God for mercy. He is unable to take the rudder and correct the vessel's attitude.

Pierre Cruzatte threatens to shoot Charbonneau if he doesn't act instantly. Charbonneau acts. Cruzatte also orders some of the men to begin bailing while others frantically row for shore. Cruzatte's quick thinking saves the vessel and it lands on shore barely above water.

Just in time Captain Lewis realizes the folly of his plan to dive into the raging river to swim to the aid of the vessel. The three-hundred yards of high waves and powerful currents most likely would have cost Captain Lewis his life

During this life-and-death struggle, Sacajawea remains in the back of the sinking vessel grabbing valuable articles as they float from the boat. She catches nearly everything. After all the recovery work is completed that evening, Captain Lewis consoles everyone with a serving of spirits.

This incident happened over 2200 miles from St. Louis. The most precious cargo the expedition had was on this boat. Sacajawea shows her calm and poise in time of great danger. Her life and her son's life is in jeopardy but she maintains her composure and saves many of the expedition's precious bundles. This

The pirogue is in danger of sinking. Sacajawea grabs valuable articles as they float from the boat.

teenage woman hanging over the gunwales of a sinking boat to rescue cargo from the wild river must have been a dramatic sight. Expedition members would certainly be impressed by the actions of the Shoshoni woman.

❖ The next day, May 15, is spent trying to dry the soaked cargo. A cloudy and damp day slows progress.

Thursday, May 16, 1805 Captain Lewis
The day is fair and warm. By 4 P.M. almost everything is dry, repacked, and ready to go. Medical supplies suffered the most damage. Other losses include garden seeds, a small amount of gunpowder, and some culinary items. Sacajawea demonstrated fortitude and resolution equal to that of any man on board the stricken craft. She saved most of the bundles which had been washed overboard.

This entry leaves no doubt about Captain Lewis's respect for the teenage Shoshoni mother. The same respect must have been shared by Captain Clark and the other men. Mature beyond her years, Sacajawea learned great survival skills in a culture that required everyday use of them.

❖ The explorers report fewer sandbars in the river. It has narrowed greatly and now has a gentle, steady current. There is constant toil against the current, using oars, towlines, and even sails when they can catch a favorable wind.

Captain Clark reports a close call with a rattlesnake.

The expedition is nearing the present-day site of Fort Benton, Montana. One of the least changed sections of the Missouri River, between Fort Benton and Fort Peck, it is today designated "A Wild and Scenic River."

Monday, May 20, 1804 <u>*Captain Lewis*</u>
*A beautiful stream about fifty yards wide is given
the name Sacajawea or Bird Woman's River.*

**Just six days after she rescues critical cargo
while under a threat to her life and the life of
her child, the explorers honor Sacajawea by
naming a beautiful river for her. Bird Woman
is Sacajawea's name in the Hidatsa language.
Her name is spelled more than ten different
ways in the journals.**

❖ The explorers report the first sightings of bighorn sheep. They
also report seeing mountains on the horizon both north (the Little
Rocky and the Bear Paws) and south (the Judith Range) of the Missouri River. As Captain Lewis writes about the great beauty of the snow-
capped mountains, he also wonders just how much of a barrier they
will be in the attempt to get to the Pacific Ocean before winter sets in.

Wednesday, May 29, 1805 <u>*Captains Lewis
and Clark*</u>
*A large abandoned Indian camp is discovered.
Moccasins are found in the camp and shown to
Sacajawea who says they were not made by her people. She thinks they belong to a tribe living north of
the Missouri River and east of the mountains,
probably Crow or Blackfeet people.*

**The captains rely on Sacajawea's knowl-
edge of tribal clothing. She could tell by looking at the moccasins which tribe made them.
The expedition would encounter no Indian
people until they reached the Beaverhead
Mountains the middle of August.**

❖ The captains describe walls of limestone and sandstone over
three hundred feet high (now called the White Cliffs of the Missouri

River Breaks in Chouteau County, Montana). They describe tough going over muddy, slippery, and sometimes sharp rocky bottoms. The white pirogue has another close call when an elkhide tow rope snaps and the vessel bumps into a rock and nearly capsizes.

After one day of extremely painful labor without a complaint from the suffering men, Captain Lewis orders that a dram of spirits be issued to each one as a reward.

The rough terrain tears the old moccasins from the men's feet and time is spent making new moccasins and repairing old ones.

The captains continue their meticulous descriptions of plants, animals, geographic features, weather, and signs of Indian camps. They describe the cache made for cargo because the red pirogue will be left behind, freeing up seven men to assist with the other vessels. When the unneeded stores are buried, Cruzatte takes out his fiddle and plays some tunes. The men are extremely cheerful and sing and dance.

Monday, June 10, 1805 Captains Lewis and Clark

As the expedition nears the great falls of the Missouri River, Captain Lewis suffers from dysentery. Captain Clark reports that Sacajawea is very ill and has been bled to relieve her fever.

This is the beginning of a life-threatening illness for Sacajawea. Bleeding her was probably adding to her problem by causing her dehydration to accelerate. Some of the medical practices used by the captains were effective, but they had only a bare minimum of training and knowledge gained prior to leaving River Dubois. It is amazing that only Sergeant Floyd died during the expedition's travels.

❖ Captain Lewis describes the completion of the cache of surplus items from the red pirogue. They pull the boat ashore on a small island above the waterline and cover it with branches to prevent sun damage. Their position is near Maria's River, a river that had not been mentioned by Indians when they described the Missouri and its tributaries. Now the captains must decide which of the rivers is the true Missouri.

Tuesday, June 11, 1805 Captain Clark
The weather is cold and windy. Sacajawea is still very sick and has been bled again, which seems to help her greatly.

> The report that Sacajawea was helped by the bleeding is questionable. Perhaps other treatments which might have been used at the same time actually helped her, or just a normal improvement might have occurred in spite of the bleeding.

❖ Captain Lewis, who had left with three men to look for the great falls, has an attack of high fever and painful dysentery. He describes boiling chokecherry twigs and drinks a pint of this strong, black, bitter concoction. By 10 P.M. all his symptoms are gone.

Wednesday, June 12, 1805 Captain Clark
Sacajawea's condition has worsened. Because she is so sick, she is moved into the back of the pirogue under the canopy to protect her from the sun. That night her condition is even worse, and she is given some nonspecified medicine.

> As Sacajawea's condition worsened, the future of four-month-old Jean Baptiste was in jeopardy. Should Sacajawea die, there was no other woman available to become his caregiver. It must have been disturbing to see the young mother so sick and her tiny baby lying next to her.

❖ Captain Lewis is traveling by land ahead of the boats. He is approaching the great falls area. Again he describes the majesty of the towering snow-capped Rocky Mountains spanning the western horizon. Continually he notes their great beauty. He ponders the formidable obstacle they present to the expedition's need to pass through them and go on to the Pacific Ocean.

Thursday, June 13, 1805 Captain Clark
The morning is clear with some dew. Sacajawea
is still very ill and has been given a dose of salts.
Private Whitehouse is ill. Three men are treated
for swellings. Sacajawea is no better.

> **Captain Clark's sick list is growing. Sacajawea's condition is becoming critical and the captain begins to fear for the woman's life.**

❖ Captain Lewis describes hearing an agreeable and tremendous roaring sound. From a hillside he can see spray rising from the plains like a huge column of smoke and is convinced he is nearing the great falls of the Missouri River.

The falls are reached by noon and Lewis gives a moving description of them and the grand and sublime spectacle they present.

Friday, June 14, 1805 Captain Clark
The morning is beautiful. Sacajawea is danger-
ously ill and complains all night long.

> **When Captain Clark uses the word *dangerously*, it suggests Sacajawea is hovering near death. Normally Sacajawea would bear her pain without complaint. Her moaning and groaning indicates the severe suffering and pain she is experiencing.**

❖ The flotilla is nearing the great falls area, a major goal of the expedition.

Captain Lewis is still out exploring the area. He hurries from one falls to the next, finding each one more beautiful than the one before it. After feasting his eyes on the ravishing beauty of the falls, he rests at a place where he can see the present-day Sun River enter the Missouri River.

He descends a hill and sees a herd of over a thousand buffalo. He shoots a fat calf and plans to leave it for his evening meal. He forgets to reload his rifle. A grizzly bear creeps to within twenty feet of the captain before he sees the beast. With no time to reload and with no trees nearby, Lewis runs for his life. He makes it to the river just in time and turns to face the bear. His spear is at the ready. The bear skids to a stop a short distance from Lewis, turns, and runs off as fast as it had come.

Captain Lewis is awestruck by the spendor of the great falls of the Missouri.

Next Lewis encounters a fierce animal (probably a wolverine) just emerging from its burrow. When the animal crouches to spring at Lewis, the captain places his rifle against his spear which he had planted in the ground to steady his weapon. He fires and the animal retreats into its underground sanctuary.

Three hundred yards away, three bull buffalo came charging at Captain Lewis who holds his ground, his rifle at the ready. The bulls stop one hundred yards short of Lewis, eye the captain, turn, and gallop off.

The day is aptly described as "an enchanting dream of curious adventures."

Saturday, June 15, 1805 Captain Clark
Sacajawea is sick and despondent. Bark is applied to her skin which seems to greatly revive her. By evening Sacajawea is even worse and refuses all medical treatment. Charbonneau requests permission to take Sacajawea and turn back.

This is the first indication that Sacajawea may be giving up. Six days of worsening illness is taking its toll on her mental state. The explorers will ignore Charbonneau's suggestion that he take Sacajawea and the baby and turn back. Sacajawea's only chance to live required that she stay with the expedition.

❖ Captain Lewis, still ahead of the main party, reports good fishing. He wakes up and sees a rattlesnake coiled next to a tree just ten feet from his bed. The rattlesnake is shot on the spot.

Lewis indicates the long portage would be best made on the south side of the river where there appear to be fewer ravines and smoother terrain.

Sunday, June 16, 1805 Captain Lewis
When Lewis returns to camp in the early after-noon, Sacajawea is near death. Four-month-old

Jean Baptiste is held in the arms of his ailing mother. Lewis is extremely concerned not only for both of them but also for the expedition's need for an interpreter who can speak with the Shoshoni people.

Not far from their camp a sulfur hotspring is found and Lewis remembers that the water from such a hotspring in Virginia was used for medicine.

Sacajawea's pulse is very weak and irregular and Lewis sees twitching in her arms and fingers. Bark and opium are quickly applied to her skin. Her pulse improves. As a last resort, Sacajawea is given large quantities of the sulfur water to drink. Soon her pulse returns to normal, the twitching is greatly decreased, and her pain subsides.

Most of Captain Lewis's entry for the day centers on the treatment of Sacajawea. The presence of a nearby hotspring of sulfur water seems to be most fortunate for Sacajawea. Captain Lewis demonstrates how much he values Sacajawea by his concern for her life. He is concerned for Jean Baptiste should his mother die. The baby's life would have been left in the hands of thirty-one men. Lewis, selfishly, is also concerned for the expedition and the need of having Sacajawea speak with the Shoshoni people when the expedition needs to buy horses and hire a guide to help them through the vast mountain range that looms above them.

❖ Canoes are being readied for the start of the portage around the falls. Captain Clark takes over the portage preparation duties. Captain Lewis remains in camp watching over Sacajawea.

Monday, June 17, 1805 Captain Lewis
Sacajawea's health is much improved. Her
appetite improves and most of her pain has disap-
peared. She continues to drink large quantities of sul-
fur water. Full recovery now seems possible.

What a dramatic change in Sacajawea's health. She even ate some buffalo soup prepared for her by Captain Lewis. According to several doctors who recently read the account of Sacajawea's illness and treatment, the hot sulfur water was a key to her recovery because they felt she had become extremely dehydrated. The sulfur water would be helpful also in fighting the infection.

❖ Captain Lewis orders the five small canoes to be moved two miles up a creek that today is called Portage Creek. There the canoes are taken out of the water and prepared for the overland haul. The white pirogue is emptied and pulled up on land for storage.

As Captain Clark is out scouting the portage route, he nearly slips into the dangerous churning waters of the Missoui River and comes within inches of being washed away to his death.

Tuesday, June 18, 1805 Captain Lewis
Sacajawea walks on shore for the first time since her
illness. Her recovery is speedy as she is now completely
free of pain, has no fever, and is eating well. Her
treatment is being continued and fifteen drops of sul-
phuric acid are added to her noon medicine.

Captain Lewis did not neglect his medical treatment of Sacajawea. His personal attention, detailed writing about Sacajawea's daily

condition, and the amount of time dedicated to helping her indicates his high regard for her as a valued member of the expedition. He certainly must have been relieved to know Sacajawea would survive to care for her baby and serve as an interpreter when the expedition met the Shoshoni people.

❖ Captain Lewis describes the hiding of the white pirogue in dense willows above the water line and also the caching of excess supplies.

Captain Clark is overseeing preparations for the gruelling portage around the great falls.

Wednesday, June 19, 1805, Captain Lewis
Sacajawea continues to improve. She gathers large numbers of white apples and eats them raw. Unknown at the time to Lewis, she also ate lots of dried fish. Her fever and stomach pain return. Lewis is disgusted with Charbonneau for letting Sacajawea eat these things because he had ordered that she eat only certain foods until she had fully recovered.

Sacajawea is given doses of saltpetre to make her perspire and thus break her fever. At 10 P.M. she is given thirty drops of opium which allows her to get a good night's sleep.

Here is a classic case of a patient not following the "doctor's" orders. Captain Lewis holds Charbonneau responsible for his wife's relapse. Captain Lewis's medical instructions would have been given to Labiche in English. Labiche would have passed them on to Charbonneau in French.

Charbonneau would have told Sacajawea in Hidatsa. There could have been a break-down in communications, or Sacajawea could have gone off on her own and ignored the Captain's instructions.

❖ The portage work proceeds. Baggage is repacked in manageable bundles. The men mend their moccasins. Gunpowder packages are improved and resealed. Axles are fashioned from trees. Crude wheels are made from larger trees.

The portage will be long and tedious.

Thursday, June 20, 1805 Captain Lewis
Sacajawea is free of pain and fever and seems headed for full recovery. She walks along the shore and even goes fishing.

The relief of Captain Lewis is evident. Only four days ago Sacajawea was on her deathbed. The captain had to be pleased with his success in saving the young mother's life.

❖ The explorers report killing eleven buffalo. The meat is being dried for use during the long portage. Captain Clark returns with his report on the portage route and worries about the reaction of the Shoshoni people to the expedition. He writes that the most perilous part of the journey lies just ahead.

On Friday, June 21, all is ready for the twenty-five day portage.

Saturday, June 22, 1805 Captains Lewis and Clark
Both captains and most of the men will make the first trip over the portage route with a canoe and bag-gage. Three men and the Charbonneau family are left to tend to the remainder of the canoes and baggage.

Each portage trip was long and strenuous. Twenty-six men labored hard to roll each canoe loaded with baggage on the wheels and axles fashioned from trees. The men left behind were probably ill or disabled. Their job would be to protect the remaining canoes and baggage. Sacajawea would not be involved in the actual portage.

❖ Ground chewed up by buffalo hooves and hardened into sharp ridges make the men's feet sore and prickly pear cactus tear through their moccasins.

One day with a favorable wind, a sail is hoisted and gives great assistance to the struggling men. The captains say now they are dryland sailors.

The captains report plenty of fresh meat and large quantities of trout are caught.

Every day ends in complete exhaustion. Each foot of progress toward the end of the portage demands backbreaking labor. At every rest stop the men lie down and instantly are sleeping. They toil through hot sun, rain, and driving winds. The men are becoming a close-knit unit pulling together to reach the same goals. Captain Clark said they did difficult work cheerfully and without complaint.

For almost two weeks while the portage labors continued, Captain Lewis stays at the end of the portage route supervising the construction of his iron-frame boat named Experiment. Three men: Joseph Fields, Sergeant Gass, and John Shields are selected to construct the boat. Hides would be stretched over an iron frame to make a boat capable of carrying lots of gear and would ride high in shallow water.

Saturday, June 29, 1805 Captain Clark
The day begins with heavy rain and then turns fair. Clark takes his servant York and the Charbonneau family on a trip to the falls. Later the wind becomes extremely violent and is followed by rain, hail, lightning, and thunder.

It is too wet and slippery to walk the portage so Captain Clark decides to return to the river camp to retrieve some notes he might have lost.

The Charbonneau family and his servant York accompany Clark back to the camp. As they near the river, threatening clouds bare down. Fearing the violent wind and approaching storm, Captain Clark leads Charbonneau and Sacajawea into a deep ravine about a quarter mile above the falls. They take shelter under overhanging ledges of rock. It seems safe enough for the captain to lay his gun, compass, and other possessions under the overhanging ledges. The light rain soon turns into a torrential downpour of rain and hail. Water from the cloudburst begins to fill the ravine. Without warning raging water comes at the group, driving rocks and debris as it thunders down the ravine.

Standing in waist-high water, Clark grabs his gun and shot pouch in his left hand. With his right hand he begins frantically climbing the steep bank. As Sacajawea climbs above him, Clark occasionally gives her a shove upward because the water is rising as fast as they can climb. Sacajawea has her baby under one arm and Charbonneau is above, pulling her up by her free hand. At the most critical time, Charbonneau freezes in a state of shock.

Without his help, Clark and Sacajawea scramble to safety above the water.

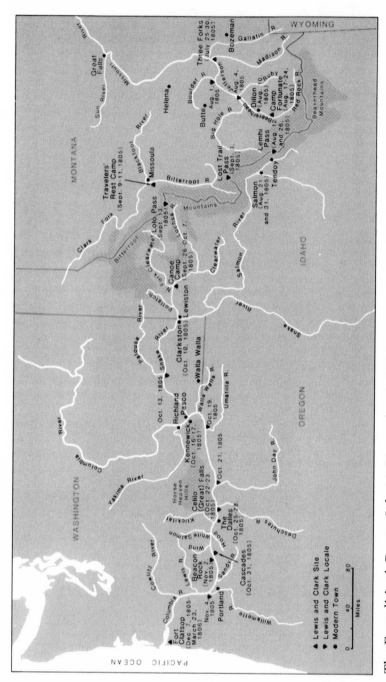

The Expedition's Route, July 28–November 1, 1805

The water is fifteen feet deep with a fiercely powerful current. Had they been swept away, they would have entered the Missouri River just above a waterfall with a drop of eighty feet.

Losses sustained by the group are: Charbonneau's gun, his shot, his powderhorn, and a tomahawk; Clark's umbrella, a gun-cleaning rod, a compass, and other items; Sacajawea lost Jean Baptiste's clothes, his cradleboard, and his bedding. Everyone is extremely cold.

York is on the plain where he had gone off to hunt buffalo just before the storm hit. He had not seen the others enter the ravine and is desperately searching for them.

At the river camp, some men are cut and bruised by the torrential hailstorm. The group dries as best it can, warms up, and is rewarded by a dram of whisky issued by Captain Clark.

Once more Charbonneau's fear of water and his ineptness during emergencies is apparent. Captain Clark, at the risk of his own life, rises to the occasion and saves Sacajawea and her baby. Sacajawea must have had Jean Baptiste out of his cradleboard and was probably nursing him or changing his clothes just before the flash flood hit. This would explain the loss of the baby's cradleboard, clothes, and bedding. This brush with death and loss of possessions is a vivid example of the hazards faced by the expedition all along their wilderness trek. For Indian women and their young, sur-

viving threats on their lives was an everyday reality. Certainly after surviving this ordeal Sacajawea immediately went to work and attended to her baby and his need for warmth and dry clothes.

❖ The long tedious portage goes on with continuous torment from hordes of mosquitoes the entire route. High winds and storms come and go. Meanwhile the men toil on without complaint. They take time to celebrate America's twenty-ninth birthday on July 4 with a dram of whiskey and a good meal. Cruzatte takes out his fiddle and the men dance.

Twenty-eight elk skins and four buffalo skins are sewn together to cover the iron boat. Captain Lewis is dismayed when he sees a problem with the stitching. The beeswax and tallow are not sealing the seams. The great venture to have a iron-framed boat capable of carrying four tons of baggage fails miserably and is abandoned. After transporting the iron frame all those miles, the expedition members are greatly disappointed.

Saturday, July 13, 1805 Captain Lewis
Lewis is happy to leave the portage camp. After he sends the canoes on to meet Captain Clark, Lewis, Sacajawea, and Private LePage (who is ill) walk three miles to the next camp.

Once again Sacajawea is with one of the captains. Also under the watchful eyes of the captains are members of the crew who are sick or disabled.

❖ Two new canoes are completed. One is twenty-five feet long and the other is thirty-one feet long. They are needed to replace the failed iron-frame boat.

On July 15 the expedition, including the two new canoes, is once more underway on the Missouri River. Total mileage gained in one month was twenty-five. It is critical now to reach the mountains and find Indian people who have horses, so badly needed to continue on to the Pacific Ocean.

Continually the captains see signs of Indian camps—but no people. Both captains write about their increasingly urgent desire to find the Shoshoni people and their horses.

Captain Clark takes three men and scouts ahead in the hopes of making contact with the Shoshoni.

Friday, July 19, 1805 Captain Lewis
Early in the morning Captain Clark finds the remains of several Indian camps. The shelters were made of willow branches and probably were used in that spring. Pine trees nearby had bark peeled from them about the same time the camp had been constructed.

Sacajawea told the captains that her people used the sap and soft wood for food.

Sacajawea's knowledge of shelters, food-gathering practices, and clothing making was very helpful to the explorers. They relied on her to interpret signs left by Indian people. (The captains shared their notes with each other. Periodically they took vacations from journal writings and caught up later as they shared experiences. That would explain Captain Lewis's account of the event even though Captain Clark discovered the camps.)

❖ Captain Clark knows he has been seen by Indian people some distance away. The Indians set fire to the prairie to warn their families of potential danger from intruders.

Sore feet and constant trouble plague Captain Clark as he works his way back to Captain Lewis and the canoes. The report is: "No success in contacting Indian people."

The expedition passes through a narrow canyon with sheer rock walls rising over one thousand feet. This spot, just north of Helena, Montana, is now called, "Gates of the Mountains."

Monday, July 22, 1805 <u>*Captain Lewis*</u>
It is eighty degrees, the warmest day of the summer. Sacajawea recognizes landmarks. She says the three forks of the great river are just ahead. This place is close to the land of her people. The men break into a loud cheer when Captain Lewis announces this news.

Each entry reveals how increasingly valuable is Sacajawea's knowledge of the land and Indian signs. She can't be credited with guiding the expedition all the way to the Pacific Ocean, but on this segment of the journey she plays an effective role in the route-finding activities. She could assure the captains the land traveled by the Lemhi Shoshoni people was the very land on which the expedition now traveled. President Jefferson's orders to follow the Missouri River to its source were being fulfilled. Captain Lewis had to be overjoyed with Sacajawea's news.

❖ When the canoes reach Captain Clark that afternoon, Lewis is shocked to find his friend with severely blistered and bleeding feet. Prickly pear cactus is the culprit. Captain Clark wants to continue on his mission to find the Shoshoni people and takes four men and once again goes ahead to seek out Indian people.

An abundance of delicious wild onions is gathered to add to the fresh venison and currants.

Wednesday, July 24, 1805 <u>*Captain Lewis*</u>
Towering mountains to the west now block the view of the expedition. Sacajawea assures him that no great waterfalls or other impassable obstructions remain

to stall the expedition but Lewis continues to worry. Surely these great mountains will present some type of obstruction.

> **Captain Lewis now realizes how vast and gigantic the Rocky Mountains really are. No wonder he fears some great obstacle. Nothing back east in the United States could compare with the mountains that now surround him and his small Corps of Discovery.**

❖ On July 25 Captain Clark and his four men arrive at the three forks area and they begin to explore it.

Once more Charbonneau has a dangerous encounter with water. Charbonneau is accidentally swept away by the current of one of the small rivers and Captain Clark has to enter the river to save Charbonneau's life.

Three days later Captain Lewis and the main party arrive at the three forks area. Extensive exploration of the three streams begins.

Sunday, July 28, 1805 Captain Lewis
The expedition leaves the headwaters of the Missouri River and follows the river coming out of the southwest. The river is named the Jefferson River to honor President Thomas Jefferson. The middle river is named the Madison River in honor of the Secretary of State, James Madison. The third stream is named the Gallatin River in honor of the Secretary of the Treasury, Albert Gallatin.

The group arrives at the exact spot where five years earlier eleven-year-old Sacajawea had been captured by Minnetare warriors. Sacajawea said her people retreated and concealed themselves in the trees when the enemy came into view. The people were followed, attacked, and some were killed. Others, like her, were captured.

Sacajawea shows no emotion and expresses no joy at returning to her homeland. She seems content wherever she happens to be. Having enough to eat and a few trinkets seem to make her happy.

> Here Captain Lewis reveals the personality of Sacajawea. Accepting of her circumstances and easily pleased, Sacajawea appears to have submitted to her captivity. With a childhood background of hunger and fear of enemy attack, she has since come to enjoy having plenty of food and possessions she never dreamed of having. Now she has her own baby and a position with a group of powerful men. The excitement of returning to her homeland seems to be lost in all of this.

❖ Captain Clark is very sick with a high fever and aching bones. Still he continues to explore the three forks area. His illness continues into a second day. He takes medicine and soaks in warm water. His condition finally improves on the third day. During the time at the three forks area, Lewis ponders the critical need for horses and realizes that without the help of the Shoshoni people in procuring these animals, the expedition may have to turn around and head home.

Tuesday, July 30, 1805 Captain Lewis
Captain Lewis, Charbonneau, Sacajawea, and the two "invalid" men walk to the exact spot where Sacajawea was captured five years earlier.

Sacajawea's capture happened close to the present-day Three Forks, Montana. It would be interesting to know Sacajawea's inner thoughts as she stands at this point again. Today, looking east from this spot one can see the highest peak in the Bridger Mountain Range. The peak is named Sacajawea Peak.

❖ On August 1 Captain Lewis with three men leaves the main party to scout ahead for a possible contact with the Shoshoni people. The captains and their men suffer from a variety of ailments and minor injuries. Boils are a constant problem, probably caused by poor diet, heavy with meat and light on fruits and vegetables.

Captain Lewis explores the Wisdom River, today called the Big Hole River. He decides to follow the other branch, now called the Beaverhead River, which he thinks is the correct route. After several mishaps and failure to find the Shoshoni, the two captains join each other for the next phase of their journey.

Thursday, August 8, 1805 *Captain Lewis*
In the evening Sacajawea points to a high formation jutting out on the valley floor. Her people called this formation the Beaver's Head because it is shaped like that animal's head. Her people come through this area every summer on their way to hunt buffalo. Soon, she says, they will find her people here, or just west on another river. The need to find the Shoshoni is becoming increasingly critical.

Sacajawea's information convinces Captain Lewis to once again leave the main party in search of Indian people. A highly excited and very worried Captain Lewis leaves the next morning. Having obeyed President Jefferson's orders to follow the Missouri River to its source, the explorers now face the seem-

Sacajawea tells the captains that her people call this rock formation "Beaver's Head."

ingly impenetrable barrier of the Rocky Mountains. If he is unable to secure horses and a guide, Captain Lewis knows he may have to turn back.

❖ Many geographic features in this area now bear the name Beaverhead: Beaverhead County, Beaverhead River, Beaverhead Mountains, Beaverhead National Forest.

Captain Lewis, Drewyer, Shields, and McNeal finally arrive at the source of the Beaverhead River. Clark's Reservoir now covers the spot. A dam, creating the water storage, was built on the Beaverhead next to Interstate 15.

From this point, Lewis and the men head west toward what is now called Lemhi Pass.

On August 11 Lewis spots a lone rider on horseback but is unable to get him to await his arrival. The man rode up and over the mountain, heading west. This is the beginning of a two-day struggle to come face to face with the Shoshoni people. There will be three sightings of Shoshoni people before Captain Lewis succeeds in making contact with an old woman and a young girl.

On August 12 Lewis and the three men cross the continental divide and unfurl the American flag. They are the first persons from the United States to cross the great divide.

On August 13 the four men are warmly welcomed by sixty mounted warriors, one of whom is a principal Indian chief named Cameahwait. The warriors had come out expecting to meet an invading enemy. Lewis was very fortunate that the Lemhi people looked on him as a friend and gave him a hearty welcome to their land. Now Lewis, through sign language expert Drewyer, would have to convince the Lemhi people to accompany Lewis on the forty-two-mile trip back to meet Clark and the rest of the men.

Wednesday, August 14, 1805 Captain Clark

Charbonneau strikes Sacajawea while the family is eating the evening meal. Clark reprimands him.

Both captains noted this incident in their journals, (Clark reported it to Lewis), indicating that both men were disgusted with Charbonneau for his abuse of Sacajawea. It probably was not the first or only time she was mistreated by her husband. This incident leaves Charbonneau with a tarnished reputation among journal readers and historians.

❖ Captain Clark and the main party continue pulling, poling, and dragging the canoes over rocks and gravelbars in the shallow Beaverhead River. Captain Clark joins the men in the water in the effort to move upstream.

The two captains had agreed to rendevous at the source of the Beaverhead River. Captain Clark was doing everything he could to make it to the designated meeting place. Captain Lewis had left a note there for Clark to mark the meeting place and had asked him to wait there for Lewis to return.

Thursday, August 15, 1805 Captain Clark
While Clark was walking on shore he has two close calls with rattlesnakes. Sacajawea is nearly bitten by a rattlesnake. So the nearby mountain receives the name, Rattlesnake Mountain.

Sacajawea must have been aware of the dangers all about her. She would be on guard and especially alert to protect herself and Jean Baptiste from constant hazards.

❖ Meanwhile, in the Lemhi Valley Captain Lewis stalls for a few days, hoping to give Captain Clark and the canoes time to reach the meeting place.

There are detailed references to the interaction with the Lemhi Shoshoni. Using Drewyer's sign language, Captain Lewis speaks to them over and over about promises of peace, gifts of wonderful things, and no more hunger if only the people will help the expedition. He also asks many questions about the Lemhi River and a larger river to the north. Possible passages through the mountains by either water or horseback are also discussed.

The Lemhi Shoshoni are very suspicious of Captain Lewis's request that they leave the safety of their valley and follow him east to the Beaverhead River. The Shoshoni fear a trap and a sneak attack by their enemies. Only a month before they had suffered an attack. Finally a small contingent of Indian people set out with Lewis and his three men to find Captain Clark.

Friday, August 16, 1805 <u>*Captain Lewis*</u>
The Indian people become very nervous as the group approaches the Beaverhead River. They arrive at the announced meeting place and the canoes are not there. Cameahwait is assured that he will soon see that Captain Clark has a woman with him who is from the Lemhi Shoshoni nation. She had been captured by the Minnetares. This woman can speak Shoshoni and would help explain the purpose of the expedition.

Now with a meeting so close to reality, Captain Lewis fears the Shoshoni will withdraw and refuse to go on because of their suspicions of a conspiracy Lewis may have with their enemies. Only twenty-eight men and three women had dared to venture out of the Lemhi Valley with these strange men. Captain Lewis uses the presence of Sacajawea to pacify the chief and his people.

❖ When Clark was not at the designated meeting place, some of the Indian people back away and take up places of self-defense in case of attack. Captain Lewis gives his own rifle to Chief Cameahwait, telling him to use it to shoot Lewis if this is treachery. Lewis mentions York, describing his black skin and short curly hair. The Indian people decide to trust the captain and camp with him for one night.

That night Lewis and Cameahwait lay side-by-side to sleep. Lewis sleeps very little as he ponders the fact that the success of the expedition now depends on the whims of the Lemhi Shoshoni people. The next day will be a critical turning point in the great venture that had already required so much preparation and toil.

Saturday, August 17, 1805 <u>*Captain Lewis*</u>
Lewis arises early. Cameahwait and Lewis agree to send Drewyer and a Lemhi Shoshoni

warrior down the Beaverhead River to find Captain Clark and the main party.

Two hours later the warrior returns and announces that the white men are close. Soon Captain Clark arrives with Charbonneau and Sacajawea.

There is an emotional reunion between Sacajawea and one of the Indian women. The two teenagers see one another and run to greet each other with great celebration. Sacajawea says that when she and her friend were eleven years old, they were captured by enemy warriors and taken to be sold as slaves. Her friend escaped and made her way home by herself.

The captains begin their meetings with the Indian people after a camp is set up. Sacajawea, Charbonneau, and Labiche serve as interpreters.

As Sacajawea begins to interpret, suddenly she recognizes her brother Cameahwait. She runs to him. They embrace. Sacajawea is in tears and throws a blanket over their heads. It is sometime later before she is composed enough to continue.

Once again the Shoshoni are told of the expedition's purposes and the need for horses and a guide. Over and over the captains promise the Shoshoni protection from their enemies, rifles for hunting, and all the wonderful things trade with the United States will bring. The captains promise to trade valuable items for each horse the expedition needs. After the

Sacajawea has an emotional reunion with a girlhood friend who also was captured by enemy warriors. They had not seen each other for over five years.

meeting all the Indians are given gifts and are fed a hearty meal.

Lewis and Clark form a plan for the critical days ahead. Clark will take eleven men and the tools needed for constructing canoes and head for the Lemhi Valley forty miles to the west. Sacajawea and Charbonneau will travel with Captain Clark and arrange to return to Captain Lewis with more of Sacajawea's people and a large number of horses. Captain Lewis will then trade for the horses, load all the baggage, and proceed to the Lemhi Valley to join Captain Clark.

> **This had to be a day of great emotion for Sacajawea. Her childhood friend, her brother, and all of her people greet her with great surprise and affection.**

❖ Captain Clark leaves for the Lemhi Valley with men and tools for building canoes should they find a navigable river nearby. The Charbonneau family goes with Clark. Captain Lewis continues to entertain the Shoshoni people and repeat over and over his promises. He tells them that if they help the explorers through the mountains, the expedition can return to the United States and soon the wonderful promises will begin to come true.

The need for horses and a guide are emphasized again and again by Captain Lewis. The Lemhi Shoshoni appear to be pleased with the words of Captain Lewis. August 18, 1805 was Captain Lewis's thirty-first birthday. For him it is a truly happy day, considering his successful dealings with the Lemhi Shoshoni. However, the humble captain laments about a life lived so far without any great accomplishments to point to.

Monday, August 19, 1805 <u>*Captain Lewis*</u>
The Shoshonis have a custom that a young girl's father promises his daughter in marriage when she is still an infant. The man who will receive a girl pays for her, usually with horses or mules. At about fourteen years of age the girl is given to her purchaser.

Sacajawea had been sold as an infant. The man who purchased her is present when she returns with the expedition. He is twice Sacajawea's age and already has two wives. Since Sacajawea had a child by Charbonneau, the Shoshoni is no longer interested in her.

> **This could have developed into an awkward situation. Sacajawea's vulnerability is apparent. What if the man claimed Sacajawea? She certainly existed in a male-dominated society. First she is promised in marriage while still an infant, then she is captured and sold to Charbonneau. Now she could be claimed by another man.**

❖ Captain Clark describes purchasing three horses with some handkerchiefs, a shirt, a pair of pants, and a few arrow points. The captains learn that when using beads for trade, blue is the color preferred by nine out of ten Indian people.

Captain Lewis describes in great detail, page after page, the Lemhi Shoshoni people, their dress, their physical features, their shelters, their food, their customs, and their beliefs.

August 20, 1805 <u>*Captain Clark*</u>
Old Toby is retained as a guide to lead the party north. The man and his son agree to accompany the expedition all the way across the mountains. Charbonneau and Sacajawea are sent back up over the

pass with more people and a good number of horses to
carry expedition baggage into the Lemhi Valley.

The Charbonneau family is given a critical task by the expedition. Captain Lewis is in dire need of horses. The journey back to the Beaverhead River where he waits is a forty-mile trip.

❖ Captain Lewis describes the caching of excess expedition baggage, done in secret lest the Indian people help themselves to expedition supplies. The plan is to retrieve the valuable items on the return journey.

Lewis is impressed by how well the Lemhi Shoshoni conduct themselves. The women work hard repairing expedition moccasins and making new ones to replace those beyond repair. Lewis spends six days at the camp before he is ready to head west to meet Captain Clark in the Lemhi Valley.

Thursday, August 22, 1805 Captain Lewis
Charbonneau, Sacajawea, fifty Shoshoni men,
and a large number of women and children arrive at the
Beaverhead camp and put up shelters nearby. The
men meet with Lewis and are given more gifts. After
the meeting all the people are fed a meal of beans, corn,
and squash. Cameahwait tells Captain Lewis that,
except for the sugar given him by his sister Sacajawea,
this is the finest food he has ever tasted.

This must have been quite a scene. Well over a hundred Indian people were present. Giving gifts and feeding such a large crowd had to be a huge undertaking. Certainly Sacajawea must have been a key player in this impressive event. Captain Lewis named this place "Camp Fortunate."

❖ Captain Lewis on the Beaverhead River and Captain Clark in the Lemhi Valley each describe the preparations for the expedition's departure over land. The Shoshoni men tell Clark about the river heading north and joining a larger river which comes from the southwest. Then a larger river flows north and soon takes a sharp turn toward the setting sun. It enters a canyon that is impassable by land or water. This river is now called the Salmon River, which because of its wild rapids and narrow canyon has been nicknamed "The River of No Return."

Captain Clark explores the canyon and confirms the Indian report. Clark dispatches a letter to Captain Lewis to report his findings because they have implications regarding the number of horses needed for a long overland trip.

Saturday, August 24, 1805 Captain Lewis
Charbonneau is given trade goods to use to purchase a horse for Sacajawea.

The fact that Captain Lewis makes special provisions for Sacajawea to have her own horse is an indication of the high esteem she has earned in her own quiet way.

❖ Captain Lewis describes his party's progress in their move to Lemhi Valley. He notes that the Lemhi people already have a few out-of-date rifles, some metal knives, and a few other articles they obtained in trade with other tribes.

Lewis has high praise for the horsemanship skills of the Lemhi Shoshoni.

Sunday, August 25, 1805 Captain Lewis
Charbonneau casually tells Captain Lewis that he expects to see the Indian people leave to go on a hunt on the Missouri River. This shocks Lewis and means that he and his baggage will be left and the

expedition stranded without horses. A crisis of major proportions looms.

Sacajawea tells Charbonneau this disturbing news early in the morning but Charbonneau waits until afternoon to tell Lewis. After letting Charbonneau know about his unhappiness over the delay in receiving this critical news, Lewis immediately calls the chiefs together to pressure them to change their plans. He reminds them of their promise to trade horses and repeats all the promises of wonderful things which will come to them if they cooperate. Fortunately he succeeds in convincing them to stay, postpone their hunt, and help the expedition.

Sacajawea had heard her people planning their departure. She immediately tells her husband. After an inexcusable delay, Charbonneau tells Captain Lewis. A devastating disaster is narrowly averted.

Some historians have said the Lemhi Shoshoni plan to abandon the explorers is treachery. That might be the view of the non-Indian. As for the Shoshoni people, one month previous they had been attacked while trying to get to the buffalo hunting lands. Now with winter drawing near and the prospect of no buffalo meat for their families, they decide to give priority to the need for food. It was simply putting the welfare of their people first. Who could fault them for that? This is not treachery.

Cameahwait certainly would have understood who the informer was. Only Sacajawea understood the Shoshoni language. She was the only one that could have overheard the

Shoshoni plans to leave for buffalo hunting grounds. This means that Sacajawea has definitely severed her ties with her people and intends to remain loyal to the expedition. It was definitely a turning point for her and for the Corps of Discovery.

❖ Finally the horse trading is completed. Captain Lewis and the main party head north to meet Captain Clark. The men are elated to be finished with their upstream struggles. The captains describe their progress from the Lemhi Valley, up rugged mountains covered with thick timber, over a high pass now named Lost Trail Pass, and down into the Bitterroot Valley of present-day Montana. There they meet the Salish people who prove to be friendly and generous—some of the finest people they meet on the entire journey. Some splendid horses are added to the expedition's herd.

At Travelers' Rest, eighteen miles south of today's Missoula, Montana, the expedition pauses.

On September 11, the torturous trip over the Lolo Trail begins. This would prove to be the toughest part of the whole journey. The expedition was reduced to eating horses and dogs.

Captain Clark and an advance party reach Weippe Prairie on Friday, September 20, 1805. There Clark sees three Nez Perce boys who run and hide. Eventually the boys come out of hiding to receive some gifts. Soon the Nez Perce adults arrive to investigate, and the association with the Nez Perce people begins.

Old Toby is spotted heading east, not even waiting to receive the pay for his guiding services. Old Toby was a key element in the success of this great expedition.

Sunday, October 13, 1805 <u>*Captain Clark*</u>
The presence of Sacajawea with the expedition convinces all Indian people of the peaceful intentions of their party. Having a woman with the expedition is a sure sign the expedition is not a war party.

The explorers continue to note Sacajawea's calming influence on tribes all along their route. Without her, threatened warriors could easily have attacked impulsively. The small group of explorers could have easily been overcome by a larger force. And usually they were greatly outnumbered by native people. Taking the expedition's rifles and goods certainly would have been tempting to needy tribes.

On the Lolo Trail, the most difficult segment of the journey.

❖ From Travelers' Rest to Nez Perce country is 160 miles of tor-turous journey but the expedition makes it in eleven days. The Nez Perce people greatly assist the expedition. They give food, assistance in building canoes from large trees, and agree to take care of the expedition's thirty-eight horses over the winter months.

Many of the men experience stomach ailments and other assorted troubles. As the illnesses spread, the expedition has all the appearances of a hospital. Captain Lewis is completely dis-abled for days with an intestinal ailment.

On October 6 the canoes are finished. On October 7 the expe-dition is once more on a river and heads downstream on the Clearwater River to the Snake River, and finally to the Columbia River. Many Indian people are encountered along the way.

Saturday, October 19, 1805 <u>*Captain Clark*</u>
There is an extremely dangerous rapids on the Columbia River. To lighten the canoes, Clark has the people, including Sacajawea, Charbonneau, and two visiting Indian people, walk around the rapids.

Captain Clark approaches an Indian settlement with a pipe in his hands. The Indian people are ter-rified and are given a few trinkets to calm them down.

The instant Captain Lewis appears with Saca-jawea, the people come out of the lodges and seem completely at ease. This made possible trade between the two groups.

From terror and fear to complete calm is the difference a woman with the expedition can accomplish. The captains made this observation again and again in their journals.

❖ Over a month passes before Sacajawea is mentioned again. The explorers describe their journey down the Columbia in their usual manner. Cold rains drench the travelers day after day. Buckskin clothing begins to rot off the wearer's body. Every expedition member, including Sacajawea and her baby, had to endure constant discomfort in the miserable weather.

November 7 is a memorable day. Captain Clark wrote, "Ocean in view! Oh, the joy!"

Sunday, November 24, 1805 Sergeant Gass

The decision on where to camp for the winter is put to a vote. Captain Clark records the votes. In the list are written the votes of the black servant York and Sacajawea. Sacajawea's vote to camp near the best supply of edible roots is recorded under her nickname, Janey.

A black is given a vote. A teenage Indian woman is given a vote. This had to be a first for a United States Army Unit. Neither of these two people would ever be allowed to vote on anything back in the states. Anyone who has ever been on an extended isolated wilderness expedition, such as mountain climbing, backpacking, or the like, knows that such a group takes on its own character. A powerful bonding between the members takes place to succeed in reaching the group's goal.

❖ High winds, constant rains, and miserable cold make life almost unbearable. Visits from coastal Indian people are recorded. These tribes have many trade goods obtained from European sailing vessels which have docked in the waters off the coast.

Should a sailing vessel visit while the expedition is still on the coast, there will be the possibility that some or all of the expedition members will be able to return to the United States by sea.

The search goes on for a suitable winter campsite.

Saturday, November 30, 1805 <u>Captain Clark</u>

Sacajawea gives the captain a piece of bread made of real flour. She had stashed some flour so she would have a food supply for nine-month-old Jean Baptiste. The flour became wet and had to be used before it spoiled. Clark has not had bread for months so this is a delicious treat.

Like any responsible mother, Sacajawea was always looking out for the welfare of her baby. This had to be a well-protected supply of flour. The expedition had long since used up its supply.

Sacajawea must have earned the respect of all the men for her devoted work to meet her baby's need for food, clothing, shelter, a cradleboard, and constant protection from the weather and the chance of injury. The growing infant must have given the men a warm feeling of a touch of home.

❖ Hunters find elk in abundance, but the terrain is covered with thick growth. Constant rain makes hunting miserable. Meat is often in poor condition and rots quickly.

Tuesday, December 3, 1805 <u>Captain Clark</u>

Hunters come in with an elk. Sacajawea eats the bone marrow from two shank bones. Then she boils the bones and gains a pint of grease for her efforts.

Use of the complete animal was a skill all Indian people learned, especially the women. Men of the expedition would have discarded the bones. Sacajawea has shown them the economic use of even the bones and for Clark this is a significant indication of her skills.

❖ On December 7 construction begins on the buildings to be used as winter quarters. The fort is named Fort Clatsop after the tribe living in the area.

Another pest bothers the explorers—fleas which infest their blankets and torment them all night. After a week of feverish activity, the log work is finished. Timbers are split into boards. Rain is almost unceasing.

December 16, according to Captain Clark, is one of the worst days ever, weatherwise. It is bitter cold, pouring rain, and wind so strong that trees are toppled.

On December 17 chinking of the logs begins. Charbonneau's hide lodge is in tatters. By Christmas Day the entire group is situated in the completed buildings—a welcome relief from utter misery.

Wednesday, December 25, 1805 Captain Clark

Christmas gifts are exchanged among the expedition members. Sacajawea gives Captain Clark twenty-four weasel tails.

A volley of shots fired by the men just outside the walls of the fort awakened the captains on Christmas morning. Following the shots, the men broke into song. This was an unusual Christmas celebration for a small band of explorers thousands of miles from home. Where did Sacajawea get her twenty-four weasel tails? Did they have a religious significance for her? Had she carried them all the way from Fort Mandan? This generous gift from a woman who had very few possessions of any worth indicates her deep respect for

Captain Clark and the spirit of giving at Christmas time.

❖ Christmas dinner is rancid boiled elk, spoiled fish, and some roots. Captain Clark calls it a bad Christmas dinner.

On December 28 the men begin building a second camp right on the seacoast. A fire is built there to burn all winter long as sea water is boiled to obtain salt. For three months the fire is fed and precious salt is gathered for use by the expedition and as a trade item on the homeward journey.

Fort Clatsop, quarters for the expedition during the winter of 1805–6.

The new year is welcomed with another volley of rifle fire. The only beverage available to toast the new year is water. Every man feels the joy of knowing the new year will find them returning home.

Monday, January 6, 1806 Captain Clark
After breakfast two canoes are readied for a trip to the ocean. Sacajawea is eager to go with the party to see the "great waters." She has traveled a long distance and she wants to see the ocean and the enormous fish that live there. She is given permission to go.

Sacajawea shows a normal curiosity. Certainly she had come so far that another short canoe trip wasn't reason enough to miss such an opportunity. Seeing the ocean and whales would be a highlight of her life. Good fortune awaited the young mother. A giant blue whale's body over a hundred feet long had washed up on to the beach.

❖ Three months pass before Sacajawea is mentioned in the explorer's journals again. The captains make lengthy entries about Indian people, daily events, and the fact that they see no ships along the coast. The captains try to maintain a routine for the men and post a constant round-the-clock guard against theft by visiting Indian people. All visiting natives leave the fort at dark and the gates are secured for the night.

The men ache for the day the trip home will begin. There are only eight days of sunshine the entire winter. All the men are bored, many suffer illness, and their diet is the same day after weary day. Healthy men are busy preparing for the trip east.

Finally at 1 P.M. on Sunday, March 23, 1806, the expedition bids farewell to Fort Clatsop. Once again the group heads upstream with their canoes.

Indians along the way charge high prices for food, some Indians steal expedition property, and even Captain Lewis's dog, Seaman, is taken. An enraged Captain Lewis orders his men to shoot to kill to get his beloved dog back. Fortunately the dog is retrieved without a shot being fired.

The third week of April the expedition leaves the Columbia River, just east of a deep gorge now officially named The Dalles, and proceeds by land to Nez Perce country. The expedition is forced to pay high prices for horses to carry their baggage and to have a few extra horses for disabled men to ride.

Wednesday, April 23, 1806 Captain Clark
The expedition meets with Indian people at the
Wah-how-pum Village. Charbonneau is able to
purchase a horse by giving a man his own shirt and
two of Sacajawea's dresses.

This is an interesting transaction. Charbonneau probably was able to use two of Sacajawea's dresses in the deal without her agreeing to give them up. Such was the status of an Indian woman in Sacajawea's position.

❖ Dogmeat becomes preferred for food over horsemeat. Dogs were purchased all along the Columbia River as a food source for the expedition. Trades were made for additional horses along the way. Indian people bring their sick to the captains for medical treatment. A long line of those in need of help forms every morning at the explorer's camp.

Monday, April 28, 1806 Captains
Lewis and Clark
A meeting is held with Walla Walla Indians. A Shoshoni woman is living with them as their prisoner.

Sacajawea serves as an interpreter as the explorers spend several hours explaining the purpose of the expedition's travels. The Walla Walla are pleased to hear the news brought by these strange men and they bring their sick and injured for treatment by the captains.

**Here is another example of Sacajawea helping the explorers make effective use of their time communicating their purposes to Indian people, as President Jefferson had instructed them to do.
It was not uncommon for an Indian woman to be taken as a prisoner to be traded away as a slave.**

❖ The expedition reaches the Snake River on May 4. They proceed on to Nez Perce country, only to learn that they must wait for nearly another month for the snows to melt to make the mountains passable.

Camp is made near present-day Kamiah, Idaho. Again Captain Clark becomes a popular physician for scores of Indian people with a variety of ailments.

Sunday, May 11, 1806 Captains Lewis and Clark

The captains and the interpreters have a meeting with the Nez Perce Indians who have a Shoshoni boy living with them. The translation went from Nez Perce to Shoshoni to Hidatsa to French to English and back. A half day is spent telling the Indian people the purpose of the expedition and what the expedition needs from the Nez Perce.

The son of a great Nez Perce chief says his father had been killed in battle. The young man believes the explorers' promises of peace among all people and says his heart is happy. In gratitude for their words, he gives the captains a beautiful mare and her new colt.

Translating back and forth through five languages was certainly slow and tedious but paid good dividends in the end. The patience shown by Lewis and Clark was rewarded time and again.

The young man is an example of most of the Indian people who listened to the captains' promises. The response was trust and hope. Certainly a teenager like Sacajawea also thought the captains were truthful and must have longed for the day her own people would benefit from all the good the great white chief in the United States would do for all people. Can anyone fault Sacajawea for her acceptance of the words of such powerful and compassionate men?

❖ The Nez Perce men begin the return of the expedition horses left with them the previous fall. Captain Lewis spends most of his time talking with Indian chiefs while Captain Clark serves as doctor for the long lines of sick waiting at his shelter each morning.

Friday, May 16, 1806 <u>Captains Lewis and Clark</u>

Sacajawea gathers a large supply of fennel roots (which were most likely Gairdner's yampah roots). The roots have an anise flavor and are tasty and nourishing. The great abundance of wild onions make a healthy addition to their diet. The onions are boiled with meat.

These roots are plentiful today along the low meadows near streams in the Kamiah, Idaho, vicinity.
Sacajawea's food-gathering skills continue to impress the explorers. The food she finds is a valuable addition to the nourishment of the men and improves their general health.

❖ Snow is still falling in the mountains. Every warm day the river rises and hopes are raised for the signal to head east soon. The men can hardly contain their excitement and eagerness to get on with the trip.

Sunday, May 18, 1806 <u>Captain Clark</u>
Sacajawea spends lots of time gathering yampah roots. She dries them so they can be taken on the journey through the mountains. The roots are tasty roasted, boiled, or dried.

Even with fifteen-month-old Jean Baptiste to care for, Sacajawea finds time to gather, dry, and store food.

❖ The wait goes on for the snows to melt off the high ridges. The rain comes regularly. The men are forced to build watertight shelters of willows and grass. When the shelters are finished, Captain Lewis says they can finally sleep warm and dry for the first time since they left Fort Clatsop.

The Nez Perce horses impress the men. The Nez Perce selectively breed their horses for speed and horse racing is a number-one pasttime of the young men. Foot races are also popular. One Nez Perce man was very fast and almost able to beat the expedition's fastest sprinters, Drewyer and Rubin Field.

Thursday, May 22, 1806 Captain Lewis
Sacajawea's baby is ill. Jean Baptiste is cutting teeth and has developed a high fever with a swollen throat. The child is given a dose of cream of tartar and flour of sulphur. A poltice of boiled onions is applied to his neck.

This is the first indication that the youngest member of the expedition is sick.

❖ The captains do everything they can to help the young boy. Daily reports appear in their journals concerning his illness, treatment, and progress.

May 23—treatment for Jean Baptiste continues all through the night. His condition seems much improved in the morning.

May 24—the child has a bad night. In the morning the boy's throat seems more swollen than before, but his fever is down.

May 25—the child's condition is worsening steadily. In the evening the captains give him an enema.

May 26—Jean Baptiste's condition improves. His fever is gone and the swelling is down.

May 27—the child's health improves as treatment is continued.

May 28—all of the child's symptoms are disappearing. A full recovery is expected.

Thursday, May 29, 1806 Captains Lewis and Clark
The child is near complete recovery. Treatment continues until June 8 when they finally declare him healed.

The captains are up at night treating a sick child. They record his daily condition, and they try a variety of treatments to help him recover. It is obvious that they have a great

concern for the welfare of their youngest
expedition member.
Modern doctors reading the captains'
description of the child's illness suspect he
had mumps or tonsillitis. Fortunately the
expedition was not moving during this time
so Jean Baptiste could receive so much
attention.

❖ During the child's illness, preparations for the expedition's
departure and trip over the Lolo Trail continue. Dried meat and
a good supply of roots are accumulated. Sixty-five horses are
ready to go. So are the men.

Captain Clark continues to treat many Indian people who seek
his help with their health problems.

On June 10 the expedition is finally on the move again, only to
be turned back a week later by deep snow on the higher eleva-
tions. A discouraged Captain Lewis writes that this is their only
retreat for the whole trip. The misery is multiplied by an all-night
downpour of cold rain.

On June 24 the expedition starts east once more. Three young
Nez Perce men are hired to guide the expedition over the Lolo.
The guides prove their worth as the expedition reaches Traveler's
Rest in the Bitterroot Valley in just six days.

Wednesday, June 25, 1806 Captains
Lewis and Clark
*At this stop on the Lolo Trail Sacajawea
gathers roots that her people eat. The root is similar to
the Jerusalem Artichoke and has an excellent flavor.*

This is another recording of Sacajawea's
knowledge of edible plants. From the captains' description we believe it is the western
spring beauty. The root is small and tasty.
Later Captain Lewis collects a few specimens
to take back with him.

❖ The highly motivated expedition members are up early every morning and on the way, headed home. The men push hard over the rough terrain and long distances are traveled each day. Finding grass for the horses is a priority. The snow-covered rocky areas, although slippery, protect the horses from the sharp rocks.

One camp is made at the Lolo Hot Springs, which is a resort today.

The young Nez Perce guides prove to be outstanding. Without them the expedition might have had to wait another month to cross the trail.

Tuesday, July 1, 1806 Captain Lewis

At Traveler's Rest plans are made for the expedition to divide into three separate groups for the return east.

Lewis will take six men and go northeast to explore the Maria's River drainage.

Clark will head south with the rest of the expedition members to retrieve cached supplies and canoes.

At the cache location Sergeant Orday will take nine men and float to the headwaters of the Missouri River and down the Missouri to the confluence of the Yellowstone River.

Captain Clark will take the Charbonneau family and the remaining eight men. From the three forks area, the headwaters of the Missouri River, Clark will cross overland due east to the Yellowstone River. He will follow the Yellowstone River until he finds trees large enough to make canoes to use for the float on the Yellowstone to the Missouri River.

Just south of the confluence with the Yellowstone River, the three parties will meet and continue on together to St. Louis.

At Traveler's Rest the expedition takes a final rest, does some hunting, and prepares to separate and head for home. Lewis describes the bitterroot plant that grows in abundance in the valley. This beautiful valley in western Montana is now called the Bitterroot Valley. The Charbonneau family stays with Captain Clark for the journey south. There would be no contact with the Lemhi Shoshoni people on their trip to the site of Camp Fortunate at the headwaters of the Beaverhead River, the place where Sacajawea first met her people on August 17, 1805.

Thursday, July 3, 1806 Captain Clark
The journey home begins with Captain Clark taking the Charbonneau family and nineteen men south up the Bitterroot Valley toward Lost Trail Pass. Sacajawea would once again prove her value as an interpreter.

Sunday, July 6, 1806 Sergeant Ordway
In the Lost Trail Pass area Sacajawea helps direct them east toward the Big Hole Valley.

Captain Clark's party would take a much shorter route east to the source of the

Beaverhead River and the expedition's cache. Here again Sacajawea's knowledge of the area helps save valuable time and effort.

❖ On July 7 Captain Clark's party stops in the Big Hole Valley at the site of a boiling hot spring. The area today is Jackson, Montana. The water is so hot (about 140 degrees) that meat can be boiled in it.

From the Big Hole Valley the expedition travels beyond present-day Bannack, Montana, over a pass, and into the Beaverhead River drainage.

On July 8 the party arrives at Camp Fortunate. Their canoes and supplies are in perfect order.

Wednesday, July 9, 1806 Captain Clark
Sacajawea shows him an edible root which resembles a carrot (probably a lomatium).

Most of the entries recorded about Sacajawea indicate her food gathering abilities. In the journals she is often called "the Squar" (Clark's spelling of Squaw), a term which today would be derogatory and politically unacceptable. In 1806 it was common usage.

❖ Sergeant Pryor takes the horses as the party's baggage is put in the canoes and the group travels down the Jefferson to the three forks area. Pryor is told to try to make camp with the group each night.

The group passes camps they used in 1805 as they headed upstream for Camp Fortunate.

Sunday, July 13, 1806 Captain Clark
The departure of Sergeant Ordway and his nine men is recorded. Ordway takes the canoes and heads down the Missouri River. Clark takes the

remaining eight men and the Charbonneau family plus forty-nine horses and a colt and heads east over land to the Yellowstone River. A letter from Clark to Lewis is sent on with Ordway should Ordway meet Lewis before Clark does.

Sacajawea, as usual, accompanies one of the captains.

❖ Clark's party travels by horseback, but looks forward to the construction of canoes and a speedy comfortable float down the Yellowstone River to the Missouri. Soon the horses would no longer be needed. The plan was to drive the horses to the Mandan-Hidatsa villages for trade with the people there.

Captain Lewis continues his exploration of the Maria's River above the great falls. The group has an unfortunate skirmish with a party of Indians that results in the death of two Indians and a hasty retreat by the captain and his men follows.

Monday, July 14, 1806 Captain Clark
Sacajawea says there is a large road leading through a pass and down to the plains where her people go to hunt buffalo. Her people would hunt for a few days and then quickly retreat to the safety of the mountains before their rifle-bearing enemies could attack them.

Today this pass is called Bozeman Pass and is the site of Interstate 90 between Bozeman and Livingston, Montana. The young Sacajawea must have accompanied hunting parties to this area. On hunting trips girls and women would be required to help harvest the meat and hides from the kills the hunters would make.

❖ On July 15 Captain Clark's group arrives at the Yellowstone River near the site of present-day Livingston. On horseback they follow the river until they find trees large enough to use for the construction of canoes.

Thursday, July 17, 1806 Captain Clark
The party discovers an Indian fort, fifty feet in diameter, with five-feet high log walls. "The Squar" tells him her people made these structures to defend themselves from attacks by enemies who had superior numbers and rifles for superior fire power.

Sacajawea is again the source of information about an Indian site. She may have even had to take shelter in such a fort.

❖ Charbonneau's horse throws him during the pursuit of a buffalo. He suffers a badly bruised hip, shoulder, and face.

Private Gibson falls while mounting his horse and lands on a snag which goes two inches into his thigh. He suffers greatly while the puncture wound heals.

Captain Clark continues to treat the sick and injured as the expedition nears its final days.

On July 20 the work begins on building two large canoes. The plan is to lash the canoes together so the entire party can be carried safely down the Yellowstone River. The camp is located near present-day Park City, Montana, just west of Billings.

Sergeant Pryor loses all the horses to an Indian raiding party. The men hurriedly make "bull boats" by stretching buffalo hides over wooden frames. They launch them and float down the Yellowstone River in an all-out attempt to catch up with Clark and his flotilla.

Friday, July 25, 1806 Captain Clark
About 4 P.M. they pull the canoes over to the right side of the Yellowstone River. About two

hundred and fifty paces from the river rose a remarkable rock formation about two-hundred feet high. The circumference is about four hundred paces. The top can be reached only by climbing up the northeast side; all other sides are too steep. The rock is named, Pompy's Tower, and a nearby creek, Baptiste's Creek, after little Jean Baptiste Charbonneau.

Pomp was the name given to Jean Baptiste by the explorers. The toddler was now seventeen months old. Captain Clark shows his fondness for the little boy, naming this prominent geographic feature for him. Captain Clark chiseled his own name and the date into the rock wall. It is the only visible existing mark left by the Corps of Discovery for the entire length of the expedition's journey. This must have been a happy day for the child's mother. Today the Bureau of Land Management administers this popular tourist stop near Billings, Montana.

❖ The party is on the river every morning at sunrise. Smooth progress is made and many miles are traveled each day. The excitement of being on the way home and getting so close has everyone eager to get going every morning and willing to press on until late in the day.

True to pattern Clark records the land and its features and creatures in great detail every day. His skills add much to the record of the journey.

Tuesday, August 3, 1806 Captain Clark
The group arrives at the Missouri River after traveling an estimated 636 miles by canoe on the

What a momentous day when Clark and his small party floated out of the Yellowstone River and into the Missouri. Clark could finally see familiar terrain again. The party

To honor Sacajawea's son, Pompy's Pillar, is named and "autographed" by Captain Clark, July 25, 1806.

was elated to reach this landmark on their journey home.

❖ Captain Clark reports loss of sleep by everyone in his party due to hordes of mosquitoes attacking them all night long.

Wednesday, August 4, 1806 <u>*Captain Clark*</u>
Jean Baptiste has been bitten so badly by mosquitoes that the toddler's face is puffy and swelling badly.

Mosquitoes and prickly pear cactus tormented the explorers much of their journey. Mosquitoes were by far one of their worst enemies. The child was not spared the hardships faced on the long wilderness journey but suffered only one serious illness. In all of American history never has an infant been part of such a major exploration. Never has a teenage mother been asked to pack up a two-month-old infant and set off into the wilderness with a U.S. Army expedition.

❖ Sergeant Pryor's party, minus the horses which were stolen, catches up with Captain Clark on August 8. Clark places a sign on the riverbank for Captain Lewis and his men to see as they approach Clark's location on the Missouri River. Captain Clark is eager for his friend to return.

Monday, August 9, 1806 <u>*Captain Clark*</u>
Sacajawea gives him some large crimson gooseberries and some deep purple currant berries.

Clark records yet another instance of Saca-jawea gathering food. As their hunters hunted, Indian women harvested edible plant parts for themselves and their families. The women were also experts at preserving food, mainly using the sun to dry meat, berries, roots, and seeds.

❖ On Thursday, August 12, 1806, Captain Lewis's party comes into view. Lewis lies in a canoe with a bad gunshot wound in his hip and buttocks. While hunting, one-eyed Cruzatte had mis-taken Lewis for an elk and shot him. Clark tends to his friend's infected wound immediately.

The two captains share tales of the happenings since their sep-aration on July 3 at Traveler's Rest. Now the expedition is back together. They proceeded on without incident to the Mandan-Hidatsa villages.

Saturday, August 17, 1806 Captain Clark

This is the day the Charbonneau family leaves the expedition (one year to the date Sacajaewa met her people at Camp Fortunate on the Beaverhead River, August 17, 1805).

Charbonneau is paid $500.33 for his services, for one horse, and for his leather lodge. Charbonneau indicates he wants to accompany the expedition to St. Louis. Because his services were no longer of use to the United States, Charbonneau is discharged. He will be allowed to accompany the group but no pay will be involved. Because there is no apparent way for Charbonneau to earn a living, he declines the captains' offer.

Clark offers to adopt Charbonneau's eighteen-month-old son and calls him a "butifull promising" child. Clark promises to raise the child in a manner he thinks best for him. The parents will agree to the adoption when their son is old enough to leave his mother — in about a year.

The expedition leaves the family and heads down the Missouri for St. Louis. On August 20, 1806, Clark writes a letter to Toussaint Charbonneau offering again to adopt his little son. Charbonneau is offered work and help with finances. Many good things are said about Charbonneau, Sacajawea, and Jean Baptiste, the little toddler who had given so much joy to the men of the expedition.

The time for separation had come. Captain Clark's love of little "Pomp" is obvious with his offer to adopt him as his own. Seemingly Charbonneau and Sacajawea felt this would be a wonderful opportunity for their child and agreed to the planned adoption. Eventually that adoption would become official.

❖ Along with the Charbonneaus, John Colter also receives his discharge at Fort Mandan so he can hire on with a trapping expedition heading up the Missouri River.

The explorers float down the Missouri River for more than a month and arrive at St. Louis at noon on September 23, 1806. The very much alive expedition members take out their rifles and fire a salute to the citizens of St. Louis who had given up hope for them and thought the entire contingent met with disaster.

Captain Clark makes the final entry in his journal on September 25, 1805:

"a fine morning—we commence wrighting."

The Charbonneau family leaves the expedition at Fort Mandan.

Now Captain Lewis can write his president to tell him that the assignment has been completed. The expedition had followed the Missouri River to its source, crossed the Rocky Mountains, and found rivers leading to the Pacific Ocean. Although he did not say so in his first letter to Jefferson, Lewis is sorry he could not report finding an easy portage over the mountains to a good river for more speedy travel to the Pacific Ocean.

Lewis tells the president he has returned with detailed information on the expedition's daily happenings and discoveries. He describes specimens collected.

It is estimated the two captains and three sergeants logged over two million words about their history-making expedition. There has probably never been a more meticulously documented exploration in all of American history. Certainly there has never been one with a teenage mother playing such a key role. After Lewis and Clark themselves, Sacajawea's name would become the next most prominent of all those taking part in this epic journey to the Pacific Ocean.

Epilogue

$\mathcal{S}$acajawea made a great contribution during the travel by The United States Army's Corps of Discovery and their history-making exploration of our continent west of the Mandan/Hidatsa villages to the Pacific Ocean.

She was adept at finding food. She was a symbol to native warriors that the expedition was a peaceful party of travelers. She was helpful as a source of information about the land from the Three Forks area to the Lemhi Valley. However, it is clear that her main contribution was as an interpreter when the expedition was in dire need of horses and a guide to make the critical traverse of the mountains before winter shut them off.

There is absolutely no evidence of any romantic involvement between Sacajawea and either captain or any man except her husband.

Confusion about her contribution to the expedition evaporates when the source of the facts about Sacajawea is consulted—The Lewis and Clark Journals.

Sacajawea's life after the expedition as well as her death and burial place have become a center of controversy. There are those who believe Sacajawea lived to be nearly one hundred years old. They believe she traveled extensively, eventually settled in Wyoming, and is buried at Fort Washakie, Wyoming. Their beliefs are based almost completely on hearsay evidence.

Diligent scholars, including Irving W. Anderson, have carefully researched the evidence and overwhelmingly place Sacajawea at Fort Manuel in South Dakota on December 20, 1812. The clerk of the fort, John C. Luttig, kept a daily journal of events. His entry for December 20, 1812 reads,

> This evening the wife of Charbonneau, a Snake Squaw, died of putrid fever. She was a good and best woman in the fort, age about 25. She left a fine infant girl.

The Fort Manuel site is on the National Register and is the recognized location of Sacajawea's death. There is no grave. Her final resting place was probably on a burial platform or in a dead tree.

Four months after Jean Baptiste's birth Sacajawea lay near death at the great falls of the Missouri River. Captain Lewis is credited with saving her life. In 1812 at Fort Manuel, four months after the birth of her baby girl, Sacajawea dies of "putrid fever." If Captain Lewis had been in Fort Manuel in December 1812, could he have once more saved the young Shoshoni mother?

This important evidence of the time and place of her death was uncovered after well-meaning historians had already put forth the theory that Sacajawea lived to be nearly one hundred years old.

Court documents in St. Louis show that Captain Clark officially became the permanent legal guardian of Sacajawea's children. In a report made by Captain Clark in the 1820s regarding the whereabouts of each expedition member, Clark listed Sacajawea as "dead." His report has to carry tremendous weight since he had taken over legal responsibility for her children and would certainly have known about her status.

This is one of those controversies that will never see a meeting of the minds. There will always be different schools of thought on this Lemhi Shoshoni Indian woman who has stirred the imaginations and emotions of so many people since she played her role in this great exploration.

Little Jean Baptiste "Pomp" Charbonneau went on to become a guide, a mountain man, an interpreter, a forty-niner, and a magistrate. He was educated through the support of Captain Clark, became proficient in English, German, French, and Spanish, and traveled in Europe. While on his way to a gold strike in Montana, on May 16, 1866, at age sixty-one, he died of pneumonia near Danner, Oregon.

Quick Reference Guide

For those who wish to check the references to Sacajawea in the Lewis and Clark Journals, here is a listing of the entries in this book cross-referenced to the entries in The Journals of the Lewis & Clark Expedition, Gary E. Moulton, ed., (Lincoln, Neb.: University of Nebraska Press, 1987).

The Truth about Sacajawea		*The Journals of the Lewis & Clark Expedition*	
Page	Date	Volume	Page
15	Nov. 4, 1804	3	228
16	Feb. 11, 1805	3	291
19	Mar. 11, 1805	3	312
20	Mar. 12, 1805	3	313
21	Mar. 14, 1805	9	121
21	Mar. 17, 1805	3	316
22	Apr. 1, 1805	3	327
24	Apr. 7, 1805	4	10
25	Apr. 9, 1805	4	15
27	Apr. 13, 1805	4	29
28	Apr. 18, 1805	4	52
29	Apr. 30, 1805	4	88
30	May 8, 1805	4	128
30	May 14, 1805	4	152
33	May 16, 1805	4	157
34	May 20, 1805	4	171
34	May 29, 1805	4	216
35	June 10, 1805	4	276
36	June 11, 1805	4	279

Page	Date	Volume	Page
69	Nov. 30, 1805	6	96
69	Dec. 3, 1805	6	106
70	Dec. 25, 1805	6	137
72	Jan. 6, 1806	6	168
73	Apr. 23, 1806	7	162
73	Apr. 28, 1806	7	178
74	May 11, 1806	7	243-4
75	May 16, 1806	7	264
76	May 18, 1806	7	269
77	May 22, 1806	7	278-97
77	May 29, 1806	7	302
78	June 25, 1806	8	51
79	July 1, 1806	8	74
80	July 3, 1806	8	161
80	July 6, 1806	8	167, 9:331
81	July 9, 1806	8	174
81	July 13, 1806	8	179
82	July 14, 1806	8	182
83	July 17, 1806	8	195
83	July 25, 1806	8	225
84	Aug. 3, 1806	8	277
86	Aug. 4, 1806	8	281
86	Aug. 9, 1806	8	286
87	Aug. 17, 1806	8	305

Ken Thomasma, a seasoned teacher, principal, and media specialist, now spends his time as a writing workshop leader and professional storyteller. He is concerned that children have accurate information about Americans who lived in the west before white settlers came. A careful researcher as well as a storyteller, Ken checks out details and descriptions with tribal leaders so that his material is not only historically accurate but also welcomed and appreciated by Indians themselves.

There are seven books in the popular Amazing Indian Children series. Three of the books have won the Wyoming Children's Book Award: *Naya Nuki*, *Pathki Nana*, and *Moho Wat*. The books have also been nominated for the Colorado Children's Book Award and the Colorado Blue Spruce Award. *Naya Nuki* was nominated for the Utah Children's Book Award. The books have been translated into Danish, Dutch, Norwegian, and Eskimo dialects for Greenland.

Ken, his wife Bobbi, and the younger Thomasmas—Dan, Cathy, grandson Oliver, and granddaughter Melissa—enjoy spectacular views of everchanging scenery from their homes located on the south border of Grand Teton National Park in Jackson Hole, Wyoming.

Agnes Vincen Talbot's love of the native American West began in her childhood days growing up in Boise, Idaho. After developing her significant natural talent, she moved to Connecticut, continued her art studies for fourteen years, and then returned to Boise. She is a disciplined art historian who insists on authenticity and demanding detail in her sculpture and western paintings. Her intricate illustrations in *The Truth about Sacajawea* reflect her love for the rich history of the American West.

She sculpted the beautiful bronze of Sacajawea, featured on the jacket front, for the Fort Lemhi Indian Community. It will be placed at the Sacajawea Cultural Interpretive Center in the Lemhi Valley, near Salmon, Idaho.